ENGLISH HERITAGE

FROM THE AIR

ENGLISH HERITAGE FROM THE ✦I✦R✦

NEIL BURTON

◆

PHOTOGRAPHS BY SKYSCAN

Foreword by The Lord Montagu of Beaulieu

English Heritage

St. Martin's Press
New York

All the sites photographed in *English Heritage From The Air* are in the care of
English Heritage, except Hampton Court Palace, Kew Palace and the Tower of London, which
are administered by the Royal Household and the Department of the Environment.

The publishers and Skyscan would like to thank the Custodians and other staff of English Heritage
for their help and co-operation. Skyscan would also like to thank the many landowners who
freely gave permission to fly from their property; and grateful thanks go to the staff of the
Civil Aviation Authority for their assistance at all times.

First published in Great Britain in 1989 by
Sidgwick and Jackson Limited
Published in the United States by
St. Martin's Press,
175 Fifth Avenue, New York, N.Y., 10010

Reprinted 1994

Book design and Art Direction by Bob Hook and Ivor Claydon

ISBN 0-312-03184-X

Typeset by Rowland Phototypesetting Limited,
Bury St Edmunds, Suffolk
Printed and bound in Great Britain by
BPCC Hazell Books Ltd
Member of BPCC Ltd

CONTENTS

This book contains a remarkable collection of unique aerial photographs, representing the best of England's renowned historical inheritance.

The photographs provide an unsurpassed opportunity of seeing so many historic castles, houses and ancient sites in a special low-level aerial perspective, made possible solely by new photographic techniques.

The camera portrays not only the spectacle of England's best-known monuments, but also shows their setting within the landscape. Seen from the air, Stonehenge discloses its sophisticated design as a prehistoric temple with a processional avenue. Dover Castle imposes its authority above the gateway to England. Hadrian's Wall, Rome's northern frontier, runs across hill and dale as a reminder of past glories.

Most of the properties selected for this book are looked after by English Heritage, which is responsible for the upkeep of much of England's great legacy of historic ancient sites. English Heritage also has wider roles in funding grants for the conservation of privately owned historic houses and buildings, archaeological excavations and research and advising central government on the listing and scheduling of special sites.

As Chairman of English Heritage, I am particularly happy to be associated with this extraordinary collection of beautiful colour photographs and to have worked closely with the authors in their selection.

MONTAGU OF BEAULIEU

ANCIENT MONUMENTS AND BALLOONS

he photographs in this book show a wide variety of monuments of the past, all of them the products of human activity. They range in date from before 3000 BC to the 1860s, and in character from prehistoric burial mounds to artillery platforms and monastic latrines. Almost all of them are in the care of English Heritage, a body which has only been in existence since April 1984, but which has a long pedigree stretching back for more than a century. In August 1882 Queen Victoria gave her royal assent to an Act of Parliament for the Better Protection of Ancient Monuments. In these early days the rights of private property owners were paramount and there was fierce opposition to any kind of outside interference, but the new Act established the principle that the State could take important antiquities into care or 'guardianship', while reserving the freehold of the land for its owners. It also established the idea that there should be a permanent staff to identify and investigate these antiquities. Twenty years later the Ancient Monuments Protection Act of 1900 widened the scope of the legislation to cover 'any structure or erection of historical or architectural interest, or any remains thereof', but this Act also introduced the distinction that an ancient monument could not be an inhabited building.

In the first half of this century a steadily increasing number of monuments were taken into guardianship. Most of them were prehistoric sites and uninhabitable ruins. There was a corresponding increase in the size of the staff charged with the care of these monuments. Besides the historians and archaeologists there were now scientists and architects specialising in the maintenance of ruins. Their common aim was to preserve the evidence of the history

The Skyscan balloon at Marble Hill House.

of the country and they avoided as far as possible anything which could be considered as 'restoration', and which would in any way falsify this historical record.

After 1945 the traditional view that the ancient monuments in the care of the State should consist only of mediaeval castles and abbey ruins, Roman military works and the more obvious megalithic structures, besides the royal palaces which had always been in State care, began to change. Since then industrial monuments, coastal fortifications, vernacular buildings and deserted mediaeval villages have all been taken in. Even more recently, the need to preserve those ruined and neglected examples of polite architecture which demonstrate the archaeological evidence for the changing development of English architecture since the Middle Ages has been appreciated, together with historic gardens and interiors. The other area where change has come dramatically since the last war is the way these monuments have come into the public domain. There are now more visitors of all ages, who take a greater interest in their heritage and have definite ideas about treatment and interpretation. It was to promote the public's enjoyment and knowledge of the architectural and archaeological heritage of England, and also to create a central agency concerned with all aspects of the man-made heritage of ancient monuments and historic buildings, that English Heritage was established.

Skyscan is a small private concern which specialises in low-level aerial photography, using for the purpose a helium-filled balloon. Good weather is an essential prerequisite for the operation, which demands a calm day and good light. At each site the Skyscan Land Rover, which houses the balloon and camera equipment, is turned to face the wind and the balloon inflated on its roof. Some people imagine that the photographer goes aloft with the balloon but the reality is less exciting. Helium is a non-explosive gas and much safer than the hydrogen which filled the war-time barrage balloons, but it has less lifting capacity. The 26-foot Skyscan balloon is only capable of lifting a platform which carries two cameras – a TV camera and a Rollei stills camera – which are arranged to have the same field of view. A TV link through the tethering cable relays the view to a monitor in the Land Rover, which also contains the controls of the electric motors which can pan and tilt the two cameras.

The balloon can be flown at any height up to 500 feet, whereas civil aircraft are normally prohibited from flying so low. It can also remain aloft all day, waiting for the light to be just right, and the Land Rover can be driven around a site with the balloon still tethered to it. The total absence of vibration and the stability of the platform allow the use of fine-grain film and slow shutter speeds, resulting in the remarkable clarity of the photographs.

The final adjustments to both height and position are usually made by an assistant simply holding the flying cable and moving around the site to directions from the photographer. The net lift exerted by the balloon is usually about 10 to 15 pounds and it can quite comfortably be manoeuvred around trees and rough ground, or pulled up and down, seeking the best angle for photography. On breezy days, however, a winch is used.

At the end of the operation the equipment is packed away. Helium is a finite natural resource, and Skyscan make their contribution to conservation by recycling the gas inside the balloon. Using a portable compressor the helium is sucked out of the balloon and pumped into cylinders in the Land Rover for re-use.

Revealing its subjects in a magical new light, balloon photography appears to offer an extraordinary opportunity to enrich our understanding – and hence encourage the better care – not only of ancient monuments and all historic buildings, but of the environment itself.

MONUMENTS

OF PREHISTORY

❧

rehistoric remains can be found in every part of England, and much can be seen above ground level. On the downland of the southern counties there are long barrows, tumuli, hill forts, boundary walls and settlements. The rugged uplands of the north and west bristle with the remains of hut-circles, stone rings and standing stones. In a few areas, notably parts of Cornwall, the modern walls dividing the fields follow boundaries established more than 3000 years ago. For every site visible above the ground there are ten more hidden from view, and museums all over England are full of prehistoric objects which have been turned up over the past few centuries. They range from stone axe-heads and iron swords to log canoes and a seemingly endless variety of broken potsherds. Few people can fail to be impressed by the magnificence of the stone circles at Stonehenge and Avebury, or the great earth banks of Maiden Castle in Dorset, but such monuments immediately raise questions: how old are they? what were they? who built them? We take for granted the notion of a historical framework which can provide some sort of an answer to these questions, but this is unwise. These are monuments of prehistory and their provenance can only be deduced from the things their builders left behind, and by comparison with other examples. Interpreting the evidence is the job of the professional archaeologist.

Over the past twenty-five years the pace of discovery through excavation and research has increased dramatically. One result of this quickening tempo has been a tendency for prehistoric studies to become highly specialised. This is natural, but for the non-specialist the tangle of information, often expressed in clipped and inscrutable language and published, if at all, in obscure periodicals

Winter snow and evening sunlight emphasise some of the main elements of Stonehenge, the most important prehistoric monument in Britain. At the centre are the famous group of stones, most conspicuously the sarsen stones, with some of their lintels still in place. Encircling them is the outer bank, originally about 6 feet high and broken by an entrance on the northeast side leading to the Avenue, which runs for a considerable distance down to the River Avon. Just where the Avenue crosses the modern main road is the Heel stone.

Windmill Hill is a Neolithic causewayed enclosure which crowns the top of a low hill near Avebury. Some remains have been found of an earlier settlement dating from about 3700 BC, but this was partly obliterated by a causewayed camp of about 3250. The enclosure consisted of three concentric ditches and banks, which were dug out with antler picks and rakes and ox shoulderblades. These yielded a large amount of broken pottery, flint tools and animal bones, showing that the camp was in use for over 1000 years. There is little to show what the ditches were for, and how these camps functioned. The earth works have been eroded and, as yet, not much of the area between the ditches has been excavated, but no remains of huts have been found. This view shows the innermost of the three ditches and two Bronze Age round barrows built inside the older enclosure.

and conference reports, makes it almost impossible to keep track of what is going on. This is particularly unfortunate because the new research has made some of the long-accepted theories about prehistoric England seem dubious. In particular, the idea that each major change in prehistoric culture was the result of an invasion from the Continent and that innovations always percolated from east to west and south to north is now old-fashioned. It is the more confusing because the new archaeology is built upon the old traditions, and uses many of the same key words and classifications which can also be found in the more elderly guidebooks to archaeological sites.

For ease of reference, prehistoric monuments are usually classified as belonging to either the Stone Age, the Bronze Age or the Iron Age. This 'Three Age' system was originally devised by Christian Jurgen Thomsen to guide the arranging of exhibits in the Danish National Museum, and was first published in English in 1848. Subdivision of the Stone Age, which lasted much longer than the others, into the Old, Middle and New Stone Age (Palaeolithic, Mesolithic and Neolithic) gave a total of five successive periods spanning the three hundred centuries before Christ. At about the same time the geological and biological researches of men like Lyell and Darwin swept away traditional beliefs about the origin of the human race. The accumulated evidence of associations between early stone tools and the bones of extinct animals led inescapably to the conclusion that human prehistory had lasted much longer than the 4004 years calculated by Archbishop Usher from the Bible. Fundamental to the practical study of early remains was the development of the Law of Stratigraphy, asserting that where deposits representing several phases are superimposed, the layer at the bottom will be the oldest and the layer at the top the most recent. This law still underpins all modern excavations at ancient sites.

Another nineteenth-century Scandinavian innovation in the approach to prehistory was the typological method of dealing with archaeological finds. The Swedish scholar Oscar Montelius demonstrated that for a single type of object – an axe-head or a pot – it was often possible to build up a sequence of development, starting with the simplest type. Such a system would not only establish which objects were earliest, but would also permit comparisons with similar sequences from other countries to illustrate the spread of ideas and methods of manufacture. Montelius and other prehistorians working before the First World

A section of part of the outer ditch at Windmill Hill, with two more Bronze Age barrows. At this point the bank made from the excavated soil is particularly well preserved.

War were concerned primarily with establishing basic methods of examining the past. Their great contribution was to divide the past into distinct periods, which could then be subdivided with the help of the typological method.

In the years between the two World Wars a new generation of prehistorians developed the old chronological system. Collections of similar remains were now identified as belonging to particular groups or 'cultures' and developments were assumed to be the result of contacts between different cultures. Being an island, Britain was isolated to an extent from the main European cultures and major changes, like the first arrival of farming, the appearance of beaker-shaped pots, or the early use of iron were explained in terms of invasion or the migration by new cultures into the country. There was some eagerness to give these cultures an ethnic and territorial identity; one of the best known is probably the 'beaker-folk', another is the 'Wessex culture' which flourished in the countryside around Avebury and Stonehenge. 'Thus prehistory can recognise peoples, and marshall them on the stage, to take the place of the personal actors who form the historians' troupe.'

During these inter-war years the British Iron Age was subdivided into three periods, reflecting in varying degrees the cultures associated with the two mainland European 'type-sites' of Hallstatt and La Tène. At Hallstatt in southern Austria is a massive prehistoric cemetery, whose graves produced a vast amount of objects from about 1000 BC, the time when bronze was just giving way to iron. La Tène, on the shore of Lake Neuchâtel in western Switzerland, yielded a quantity of iron weapons with curving tendril decoration of a kind usually called 'Celtic', and which could be dated to the immediate pre-Roman period. Similar weapons have been found in Britain, but the idea that these foreign cultures actually invaded is now discredited and it seems more likely that their artefacts and techniques were diffused by trade. Nevertheless, Hallstatt and La Tène have become category names and still crop up in any discussion of the English Iron Age.

Since the last war the techniques used for coaxing information about the past out of the ground have grown more sophisticated. Careful aerial photography can reveal the slightest undulations in the ground surface and allow ancient features to be picked out; geophysical surveys which look through the soil can show otherwise invisible signs of past disturbance. Computer-based systems are

*B*elas Knap is a Stone Age long barrow, which was probably built in the centuries after 3000 BC. In its original condition the barrow was about 200 feet long and 80 feet wide, built of stone and covered with a sloping roof of stone slabs. The entrances to the four small burial chambers were at the narrower south end and halfway along each side. At the north end is a much more elaborate entrance with two projecting horns and a 'U'-shaped forecourt, but this is what is called a 'false portal', presumably intended to distract the attentions of intending grave robbers from the main burial chambers. The barrow was investigated several times in the last century and altogether remains of thirty-three adults and five children have been recovered.

A closer view of the false northern portal at Belas Knap, showing the projecting horns. The inner sides of the horns are faced with dry-stone walls, of which the lower parts are original; the upper parts have been rebuilt in modern times.

ideal for storing, sorting and cross-referencing the kind of information which is produced by most archaeological 'digs', making typological analysis considerably more efficient. Numerous techniques of physical and chemical analysis have been tried on prehistoric materials, which allow their chemical composition to be determined and in many cases their place of origin to be located. An early application of this technique led to the discovery in 1923 that the bluestones which form part of Stonehenge had come from the Precelly Mountains of Dyfed in southwest Wales. The biological sciences have also made a significant contribution. It is possible to extract from samples of soil microscopic remains of once-living organisms like insects, pollen, pieces of charcoal and tiny seeds, all of which help to build up a picture of the environment to which they originally belonged.

By far the most significant advance has been the dating of sites by the radiocarbon method. Before the Second World War, all prehistoric dates had been estimates, but in 1949 the American chemist Willard Libby found a way of providing much more precise dates which could be expressed not in broad periods but in years BC. His method was based on the discovery that all living things contain a tiny proportion of a radioactive variety of carbon called radiocarbon or carbon 14. It is derived from the atmosphere through food, and intake stops at death. Like all radioactive elements, radiocarbon decays in a regular way, so that, after a fixed length of time known as the half-life, half the radioactive material has decayed and half remains. After two half-lives, a quarter remains and so on. Libby realised that since he could establish the ratio of carbon to carbon 14 in living things, and could also measure the half-life, a measurement of the amount of radiocarbon in a sample of old organic material – wood, leather, bone or earth – would allow him to calculate its age within fairly tight limits. These limits are now usually expressed as a standard deviation: a plus or minus figure after a given date, as in 1000 ±150 years. They seem wide in historical terms, but are much more precise than anything before.

Libby's method is good for material from any part of the world, but one problem has emerged. Before about 1000 BC radiocarbon years are shorter than calendar years, and give dates which are too recent. An attempt has been made to correct this by a cross-measurement or calibration based on samples of wood from the Californian bristlecone pine tree which can live to an age of about 4000 years. Fossilised specimens also exist which were alive in the Stone Age. Samples of wood were dated both by the radiocarbon method and by counting the annual growth rings in the trunk and the readings obtained in this way gave a series of corrected dates, but there is still disagreement among physicists and archaeologists about the reliability of this calibration.

The first radiocarbon dates shook established theories because they suggested that many monuments were much older than had been thought, but initial distrust of the method has been overcome and the large number of radiocarbon dates now available can be combined to provide at least an outline chronology of prehistory. Following this chronology and very broadly speaking, the Palaeolithic and Mesolithic periods extended from about 1,000,000 BC to about 3500 BC, the Neolithic from about 3500 BC to about 2000 BC, the Bronze Age from about 2000 BC to about 600 BC and the Iron Age from about 600 BC until the Roman conquest in AD 43. Of these periods the Palaeolithic and Mesolithic have left few permanent monuments and most traces of the earliest humans in this country have been wiped away by the glaciers which periodically covered the country. The occupants of the European peninsula that was Britain lived a generally nomadic life and made use of natural accommodation like caves. Few formal burials are known, but isolated human bones have been found at a number of cave sites. By about 6000 BC Britain had become an island and in the following millennia development continued uninfluenced by the European mainland.

After about 4000 BC relatively sophisticated objects like sickles and polished stone axes make their appearance, as do permanent settlements. At the core of these changes was a shift of emphasis away from hunting towards a more regular agriculture. This was the era of the first farmers in Britain; their new livestock must have been brought from abroad, but techniques could well have been copied by the existing population from mainland examples. Little survives of these earliest farms, which grew wheat and barley and herded cattle, sheep and pigs. Small settlements spread rapidly across the whole country and by about 3000 BC small villages began to appear. In some parts of Britain the single farms existed alongside large circular enclosures known as 'causewayed camps', whose boundaries consist of an earth rampart and a ditch. About fifty of them are known. Their size varies considerably and their purposes include settlements,

*W*est Kennet long barrow is one of the group of important Neolithic monuments surviving near the stone circle of Avebury. The barrow was probably built at some time between 3000 and 2500 BC and consists of a long mound flanked by two ditches. The mound is constructed of local sarsen stones and at the wider eastern end is the entrance which leads to five small burial chambers. These chambers contained the remains of over forty-six individuals. Apart from its size, the most striking feature of West Kennet is the eastern entrance. As first built there was a crescent-shaped forecourt leading into the central passage of the burial areas, but in later centuries when burials had ceased the small chambers were completely filled with chalk rubble and the forecourt was blocked with boulders. The operation was completed by placing three very large stone slabs across the front of the barrow.

Silbury Hill (see previous page), the most immediately spectacular monument of the Avebury group, is a huge earth mound about the size of the smallest of the Pyramids. The hill is also a remarkably skilful piece of civil engineering, though this is not obvious. Under the turf covering is an elaborate framework of hard chalk walls which has kept the rough chalk fill in place without subsidence or spreading for the last 4000 years. Turf at the inner core has been radiocarbon-dated to 2660 BC, though the construction work must have taken many years. Indeed, it is the huge amount of labour involved which makes Silbury so important, showing clearly that late Neolithic society in Wiltshire was capable of remarkable feats of organisation. In its original state, surrounded by a ditch 125 feet wide and 30 feet deep, Silbury must have looked even more impressive – but its function is a complete mystery and repeated attempts have failed to reveal any burials inside the mound.

burial places and meeting centres. One of these causewayed camps was at Wind-mill Hill in north Wiltshire, whose triple ditches enclose about twenty-four acres.

Throughout Britain these early farming groups buried their dead in collective tombs of stone and timber. After about 2800 BC it became fashionable to construct much larger tombs, whose principal feature was a long rectangular mound or barrow covering one or more burial areas. Among the largest specimens is West Kennet in Wiltshire which is 328 feet long. Some of these long barrows were built over existing smaller burial mounds and all of them represent a huge investment of labour, probably over a long period. Many had burial chambers lined with large stones (or megaliths) which were kept open to allow repeated burials. It is not uncommon to find the remains of as many as fifty people divided between several small chambers and apparently accumulated over several centuries. Judging by the amount of human effort expended in building the barrows, the bones inside represent only a handful of the population, presumably some kind of elite group. At one time it was thought that the idea of building such monuments had spread to Britain from the Mediterranean, but radiocarbon dating has shown that the long barrows of northern Europe pre-date similar Mediterranean examples by as much as 1000 years.

Long barrows are found, with regional variations in design, all over the country, which suggests that there was already a degree of communication between all parts of Britain. This seems to be confirmed by the wide dispersal of different types of pottery and weapons. These same objects have been inter-preted to suggest the existence of several large regional groupings with common traditions. In southern England, the Thames Valley, the Cotswolds, the Sussex Downs and the chalklands of Wessex were all intensely settled, though further north settlement was often confined to the coast and the main river valleys.

New cultural patterns emerged in the centuries after 2500 BC, especially in southern England. The change is marked most obviously by the decline of the great long barrows. Several had their entrances permanently blocked and others simply fell out of use. In their stead came much smaller round barrows, which took over as the principal burial monuments. Round barrows were usually intended to contain only one grave and from this time forward it became common practice to bury ornaments, weapons and other objects with the dead. There is considerable variety in the number and type of these 'grave goods' and

The final stage in the building of the Silbury mound was the filling-in of the stepped outline produced by the constructional walls with earth, to produce a smooth profile. For some reason the topmost step was never filled in, though whether this was intentional is unclear. In 1776 Cornish miners were employed to sink a shaft from the top of the mound to the original ground level some 100 feet below. They found nothing which gave any clue to Silbury's original function.

Two ceremonial avenues extended from the circle at Avebury; one of them runs for 1½ miles southeastwards to The Sanctuary where modern ground-markers show the position of the uprights of a succession of timber buildings. The earliest was a small circular structure at the centre of the circle, built about 2500 BC. In the following centuries it was replaced by two larger buildings and finally by an inner and outer stone circle. In this view the larger markers show the position of the stones, the smaller ones the position of the wooden post-holes. Leading away from the top of the ring are three pairs of stones which mark the beginning of the ceremonial West Kennet Avenue which leads to Avebury.

analogy with present-day practice among primitive societies suggests that the number of objects with the burial can be taken as an indicator of the wealth and status of the dead. The implication is that social distinctions had become considerably more important in the third millennium.

Pollen records show that many areas which had previously been cleared for farming reverted to woodland at about this time, which suggests that there was an alteration in the agricultural base of some parts of society. Concurrent with this change two new types of monument appear, the cursus and the henge. Cursus monuments comprise a pair of long ditches with internal banks and closed ends. There are over thirty examples in England. Their name derives from the nineteenth-century idea that they were prehistoric race-tracks, but their original purpose is unknown. Henges are circular enclosures which usually consist of a ditch encircled by a bank, reversing the usual arrangement of fortifications and making them useless as defensive works, unless the idea was to confine things inside. The great majority of henges were built during the five hundred years before 2000 BC; at Stonehenge the ditch, which is the earliest element, has been carbon-dated to 2440 ± 60.

Shortly before 2000 BC new objects began to appear among the grave goods in many parts of England. These were finely finished pottery cups known from their shape as beakers. They can also be found in many parts of northwestern mainland Europe and may have originated in the Netherlands. At one time it was thought that the introduction of beaker pottery into Britain was a clear indication of a large-scale invasion from the mainland by a new culture or people, who were characterised as the 'Beaker Folk'. Their arrival provided a convenient explanation for major cultural changes which took place in the next few centuries. Recent work has cast some doubt on this picture and there are now two schools of thought; one adheres to the invasion theory, although an invasion on a somewhat smaller scale, the other prefers to see the beakers and the new ornaments and weapons associated with them as objects of high fashion which were seized on by a native population as status symbols.

Before the arrival of beakers some spectacular earthworks had been begun in southern England. They include the huge henges at Durrington Walls, Marden and Avebury in Wiltshire and also the mound called Silbury Hill in the same county. Silbury, of which the first phase was begun in about 2145 BC, is the

The Sanctuary stands at the intersection of the modern A4 and a track which marks the line of the prehistoric route called The Ridgeway. Extending eastwards as far as Norfolk, this was one of the most important lines of communication between two prosperous parts of the country. The original importance of The Sanctuary is underlined by the fact that the sites of fifteen round barrows have been identified nearby.

largest man-made earth mound in Europe. It was carefully built, with a stepped sub-structure of chalk to prevent spreading, and the outline was later smoothed with earth and turf. All these works required a large and well-organised work-force and they mark out the downlands of southern England as an area of considerable wealth.

In about 1700 BC a new type of stone circle with widely spaced stones made its appearance in many parts of the country. At Avebury the stones were arranged within the existing henge, while at the Sanctuary, also in Wiltshire, they replaced earlier wooden uprights. There were also many brand-new circles and not infrequently these were built in conjunction with stone rows. During this period Stonehenge itself was remodelled and took on the main outlines of its present appearance. The remodelling involved first the addition of a double circle of bluestones brought from South Wales and later a ring of much larger local sarsen stones supporting a continuous ring of lintels. The sarsens were shaped, and linked firmly together by mortise and tenon joints, and the whole construction shows a remarkable degree of skill both in the design and in the putting together of the parts. The original purpose and significance of these stone circles is still as much of a mystery as the purpose of the earlier henges and cursus monuments. It has been argued that they are the product of sophisticated mathematics. This is far from being universally accepted, but there is general agreement that the positions of the stones has some relation to the position of the sun and moon at particular seasons. Stonehenge, like many other circles, provided a focus for burials and the country round it is dotted with remains of over 250 round barrows of different types. In central southern England some of the graves dating from about 1600 BC have proved to be particularly rich in funeral goods, and this has also been taken as evidence of the exceptional wealth of what has been called the 'Wessex culture'.

One of the things which must have made the building of these great monuments easier was an improvement in the quality of the tools available in the centuries after 2000 BC. The improvement amounted to a technological revolution. The quality of flintworking was much refined, and it was during this period that the flint mines at Grimes Graves in Norfolk rose to prominence. More significant for the future was the development of a competent metal-working industry, capable of casting sword-blades, spear-heads, axes and ornaments in

*T*he Avebury circle is the centre of a complex of great Neolithic monuments which also includes Silbury Hill and The Sanctuary. Their original function is unclear but they were presumably part of a religious or ceremonial centre, and all were built between about 2500 and 2000 BC. Encircling the present-day village of Avebury is an enormous earthwork, consisting of a great bank and an inner ditch which was originally twice as deep. The four causeways which cross the ditch are now used by the modern roads. Lining the whole of the inner side of the ditch was the main circle, which consisted of nearly 100 large and irregular sarsen stones. Inside the main circle were two smaller circles with standing stones at their centres. The south circle contained one called the Obelisk which was taller than all the rest. The present appearance of Avebury owes much to Mr Alexander Keiller, who purchased most of the land here, carried out excavations in the late 1930s, restored many of the stones on the west side and founded the Avebury Museum.

*T*he line of The Avenue, which links Avebury circle with The Sanctuary, is marked by pairs of stones. There were originally over 100 pairs, but at the beginning of this century only four were still standing and nine lay fallen. These have now been re-erected, together with other stones buried in mediaeval times, and the position of vanished stones in the northern part of The Avenue is now shown by concrete markers. The function of The Avenue is as mysterious as that of the other monuments.

A close view of the central group at Stonehenge, showing the larger sarsen stones and the smaller blue stones forming an inner ring.

copper or bronze – but at first these objects were not in common use. Although these technological developments were sustained through the rest of the second millennium BC, no more great monuments were begun after about 1500 BC. Round barrow burials also became less popular and there was an increase in the practice of cremation. From about 1200 BC the ashes of individuals were sometimes buried in cemeteries which often incorporated earlier barrows.

Arthur's Round Table is one of a pair of circular earthworks or henges of about 2000 BC, which stand within a short distance of one another, and presumably had some sort of connection. Unfortunately the ground between them is partly occupied by modern buildings, making investigation difficult.

*M*ayburgh is a Neolithic henge monument dating from about 2000 BC or a little later. Besides the single standing stone in the centre there were also, in the eighteenth century, four more stones in the centre and two pairs marking the eastern entrance, which faces towards Arthur's Round Table about ¼ mile away.

The site of Grimes Graves lies in the Breckland, a wild area of heath in the southern part of Norfolk. The surface of the ground is pitted with a series of hollows which are the tops of blocked mine-shafts. There are over 350 of these shafts, all closely grouped together, which were sunk in the later Neolithic period to obtain flints which could be worked up into tools and weapons. The flints here were of particularly good quality. Most of the shafts are about 40 feet deep and open at the bottom into a series of small chambers, which produced a large number of antler-picks. Grimes Graves were rediscovered in the 1870s. Their name is Anglo-Saxon: Grim is identical with the Saxon God Woden and grave is the Saxon word for a hole or hollow.

The reasons for these changes are not clear, although one factor was probably a shift of population. It seems likely that in many areas crude overfarming had exhausted the soil and made it incapable of sustaining the original good yields. This was certainly true of 'marginal' areas, whose fertility had been low in the first place, and they were the first to be abandoned. Ironically it is marginal districts like Dartmoor and the steeper parts of the Wessex downland which still show traces of second millennium agriculture today, with small rectangular fields defined by low banks. Another possible reason for changes in the pattern of agriculture and also society in the later second millennium was a marked worsening of the climate, which became both colder and wetter.

One consequence of the move away from the marginal areas was that the population density in habitable areas was increased, putting a strain on resources. From about 1000 BC there was a gradual but steady increase in the number of settlement sites with defensive walls – which may indicate that raiding and warfare were becoming more frequent. Aggression continued to be central to social relations throughout the first millennium and this is best illustrated by the very large number of hill forts, of which over 3000 have been recorded in Britain as a whole. These forts are mostly found in a crescent-shaped zone sweeping westwards from Kent to Dorset and northwards into North Wales. In the two centuries after 600 BC a rash of small defended village settlements was built in this area but with a few much larger ones which may have served as enclosures for livestock. In the fourth century BC some of these early hill forts fell out of use, but some were elaborated and extended. Danebury in Hampshire is probably the most thoroughly investigated example of these 'developed' hill forts. Its defences included a complex rampart defending the entrance, with platforms for sling-shots, while the interior was filled with round houses and storage pits. Such places probably functioned as the centre of a clearly defined area or chiefdom, and as a storage centre for the produce from a number of surrounding farms. Elsewhere in the country social arrangements and settlement patterns may have been different. Eastern England for example has produced few hill forts and the considerable population seems to have lived mostly in undefended villages scattered across the countryside.

From the fourth century BC onwards there is increasing evidence of iron-smelting. Iron had been known in Britain as early as the seventh century but it

T he Winterbourne Abbas Poor Lot barrows, forty-four of them in all, are gathered into what was evidently an important Bronze Age cemetery. Few of these barrows have been excavated in modern times, but they must date from the second millennium BC and be broadly contemporary with the Avebury monuments.

In early prehistoric times Dartmoor was a favourite area for settlement, but was largely abandoned in 500 BC as a result of over-exploitation by man. Remains of these earlier settlements are abundant on the moor, most famously at Grimspound, but also here at Hound Tor. After a gap of 1000 years the site was re-occupied in Saxon times, only to be abandoned once more in the 14th century after another deterioration in climate, and the depopulating effects of the Black Death. The visible remains are mostly of this later period of occupation.

The White Horse cut into the chalk downs at Uffington has the distinction of being the only undoubted prehistoric hill figure in England. It resembles closely the horses shown on coins minted by Belgic tribes like the Dobunni at the time of the Roman invasion and may well be a tribal emblem.

*B*elow the Uffington
horse a wide natural
valley opens out which is
known as The Manger.
Above and to the south is
the silhouette of an Iron
Age hill fort which
probably belonged to the
tribe responsible for
cutting the great chalk
figure. The fort was
placed to command the
ancient highway along
the Downs called The
Ridgeway; in this view
the great ramparts can be
seen looming on the
horizon.

The first settlement at Maiden Castle (see previous page) was a causewayed camp, which occupied the eastern part of the hill. All visible trace of this has now been obliterated. Abandoned in the early Bronze Age, the east part of the site was re-occupied in about 500 BC and the western boundary of this new hill fort runs across the middle of the present enclosure. Some time after 100 BC the settlement expanded westwards and a splendid triple rampart was built to enclose the whole. A huge cache of sling-shot pebbles was found inside the fort: presumably the defenders' supply. Despite these strong defences, Maiden Castle was overrun in AD 43 by the Roman 2nd legion under the command of the future Emperor Vespasian and soon fell out of use, supplanted by nearby Dorchester. Towards the end of the Roman occupation of Britain the east end of the fort came back into use again for a time as the precinct of a small pagan temple.

now became widespread. Most areas of England lie fairly near to supplies of iron ore and ingots of the prepared metal were traded into all parts of the country for working-up into weapons and ornaments. Trade with the mainland of Europe flourished in this period and in many cases the patterns of English products copy those of imported examples, of the kind which were found in the famous type-sites of Hallstatt and La Tène. Metalwork of the La Tène style which developed in Europe at the beginning of the fifth century BC appears in Britain very soon after. The principal English importing areas were the Channel coast and the east coast as far north as the Humber, but products from Gaul, Spain and the Mediterranean found their way into the country through the southwest peninsula as a consequence of the trade in tin from Devon and Cornwall.

Contact between SE England and mainland Europe grew closer after about 100 BC. Doubtless this was a direct effect of the expansion of the Roman Empire, which both stimulated trade and increased the importance of Britain as a haven for refugees whose countries had been conquered. According to Julius Caesar, the coastal part of southern England was occupied by a people called the Belgae, who had crossed from Belgium as invaders and had settled. Evidence for the arrival of these 'Belgic' peoples has been sought in archaeological remains, especially in distinctive types of pottery and in coins which are of a similar type to those current in northern France. But the idea of a Belgic invasion has, like the earlier invasions, become unfashionable.

During the century after Caesar's preliminary visit to Britain in 55 BC, English society continued to develop along its traditional lines, but some settlements became particularly prominent and might be described as the first English towns. Among them were Camulodunum (Colchester), Verulamium (St Albans) and Canterbury. All were in what has been called the 'core-zone' – that is to say, the southeastern corner of England which had the closest contacts with Romanised Europe. Outside the core-zone urbanisation of this kind seems lacking, but some of the hill forts were made much stronger, perhaps in anticipation of a full-scale Roman invasion, which eventually came in AD 43. Conspicuous among these late forts is Maiden Castle in Dorset, which commanded the important trade route from the harbours at Hengistbury and Poole in Dorset to the west Midlands. The defences at Maiden Castle are still immensely impressive, but in the end they did not prove effective against the Roman army.

This detail shows the very elaborate arrangement of the ramparts defending the western entrance to Maiden Castle. Erosion over 2000 years has rounded their contours, but these ramparts still look formidable, especially from the ground. Originally the route to the inner gate twisted past a series of platforms, from which hostile intruders could be bombarded with sling-shots and other missiles.

REMAINS OF ROMAN BRITAIN

he first Roman army landed in Britain in 55 BC: the nearest thing to a formal disengagement came in AD 410. During the four and a half centuries between these dates England became thoroughly Romanised, Wales and Scotland partly so. After AD 43 Britain was formally incorporated into the Roman Empire, with a governor of senatorial rank supported by a continuing military presence. In the wake of the roads and strongholds built by the soldiers, civilian settlements sprang up and remains of these constructions can be found all over the country. Unfortunately, Roman remains are not always inspiring for the casual visitor. Sometimes the sites themselves are spectacular, but the surviving walls are seldom more than a few feet high, and likely enough they will have been consolidated with recent mortar, destroying any impression of antiquity. The arrangement of the walls is often confusing because they are seldom the product of a single building operation, but rather of a series of alterations and additions over a long period, sometimes over several centuries. Besides the walls, and perhaps some enigmatic unexcavated humps in the ground alongside, there may not be much else to look at. Even after a site has been fully excavated its appearance may not change very much. Mosaic floors are usually left in place, but other visually appealing objects are most often removed to a museum. The most illuminating information about these sites often comes from fragments of Latin inscriptions, coins, slight signs of charring on the walls and other such things which need interpretation by experts. Proper appreciation of individual Roman sites requires a deal of hard reading so that the context of the ruins can be fully understood. Fortunately the planning of Roman forts, settlements and

Now marooned inland, Richborough offered the Roman transport ships their best landing place for the invasion of AD 43. Forty years later a splendid monument was erected here, probably by the Emperor Domitian, to commemorate the final conquest of Britain by his general Agricola. By the middle of the third century Britain's south coasts were being harried by sea-raiders and the monument was stripped of its marble and bronze ornaments and turned into a watch-tower defended by a triple ditch. Only a few years later, probably in the 270s, these defences were made redundant by the building of a much stronger fort with a rectangular masonry wall and ditches. It was one of a chain of new coastal castles extending from Portsmouth to The Wash and known as the Saxon Shore forts. The site at Richborough was in use for the whole of the Roman occupation, and there are remains of buildings of several periods.

villas usually followed a conventional pattern, or at least incorporated standard units of accommodation, which can be recognised by the amateur without difficulty.

Most of the Roman sites illustrated here are military, and among the others, the town of Wroxeter started life as a legionary fortress. In one sense this is clearly unbalanced, since England was extensively settled during the occupation and there are large numbers of civilian Romano-British sites to be seen. But perhaps this imbalance is appropriate. For one thing, the province of Britannia had a surprisingly large garrison, and saw a great deal of military campaigning at various times. As a result there is a very large number of fortifications of all kinds available for inspection. Indeed, the wealth of military antiquities available for study in Britain illustrates the archaeology of the Roman army in a way which is unique in the Roman Empire. For another thing, military history was much better documented than the history of ordinary civilian life. The accounts of the various campaigns during the occupation provide the best outline history of Britain during these four centuries, and one on which it is possible to build a wider understanding of life in the province. Documents like the late fourth-century *Notitia Dignitatum*, an official list of garrisons throughout the Empire giving the names of the various units and the structure of command, are of much more than military significance.

When Julius Caesar landed on the south coast of England in August, 55 BC, his intention was merely to spy out the land. During the previous three years while campaigning in northern France as governor of Gaul he must have become aware of the influence exerted by Britain on this part of Europe. There was close economic and social contact between the tribes on either side of the English Channel, and Britain offered both a refuge for fugitives from Rome and a good base for continuing opposition. Caesar and his two legions probably came ashore near Walmer in Kent. His cavalry did not arrive because of bad weather, which also damaged his ships, and precious time was spent repairing them. As a result, the troops did not get far from the coast before they were recalled to France, but at least they had overcome the physical and psychological barrier of the Channel and had encountered British chariot warfare for the first time. In the following year Caesar returned, this time with five legions and 2000 cavalry – about 30,000 troops in all. The weather again damaged his ships and delayed his

This view shows the remains of the particularly elaborate bath-house at the Roman city of Viroconium, now called Wroxeter. The town lies near the point where the important Roman road called Watling Street reached the River Severn, and it probably started life as a fortress built by the 14th legion as a base for campaigns against the Welsh. A civilian settlement quickly grew up near the fortress and, when the main Roman army base in the west Midlands was shifted to Chester in about AD 90, Wroxeter was given to the local tribe called the Cornovii as a new administrative capital. A new town was laid out on Roman lines, with a grid of streets and the amenities of civilised living, including elaborate arrangements for bathing. Major improvements were made to the original layout, especially to the forum and baths, at the behest of the Emperor Hadrian who visited Britain in AD 120. In the foreground can be seen the ornamental outline of the piscina or open-air swimming pool. To the right are the caldarium and tepidarium, marked by the red-tile remains of the hypocaust central heating system.

*C*orbridge in Northumberland was an important military settlement pre-dating Hadrian's Wall. It stands just north of the River Tyne and was intended to guard a bridge, whose remains can still be seen when the river is low. This was also the place where the road called Dere Street leading northwards joined the east-west Stanegate from Carlisle, which runs through the middle of the site. Corbridge was first established as a cavalry fort in about AD 85 after the campaigns by the Roman general Agricola in the north and in Scotland. By the 160s, after a succession of forts had occupied the site, the area was ripe for redevelopment and in the following twenty or so years, a town was laid out, but the grand scheme was quickly abandoned. Most of the north part of the site is occupied by the foundations of what may have been the intended forum or market place, never completed. On the right are two granary buildings, with flagstone floors raised on low walls to allow the free circulation of air round the stored grain. Beyond the line of the Stanegate are the foundations of a military compound.

Corbridge military settlement is a large site with work from many periods. In the foreground of this view is the headquarters building, with a temple site to the left of it and the foundations of a workshop building beyond. On the other side of the road, at the top of the picture, is the grassed area of the great storehouse left unfinished in 211 BC, while in the foreground is a collection of stone drains.

advance, but he was able to defeat an army of united British tribes under Cassivellaunus, probably somewhere near Canterbury. Caesar then pushed forward across the Thames into Cassivellaunus's own territory. Terms were agreed, hostages given, a tribute fixed and, after only two months in the country, the Roman army recrossed the Channel. It did not return for nearly one hundred years.

As the historian Tacitus later observed, Julius Caesar had revealed rather than bequeathed Britain to Rome, although there can be little doubt that even without direct rule a Romanising influence was exerted. In the wake of the campaigns, trade between Britain and the central parts of the Empire seems to have picked up; the large numbers of Italian earthenware wine containers found in the Essex territory of the Trinovantes are among the telling indicators of this development – some Britons clearly found the benefits of a civilised Roman existence attractive. During the first decades after Christ, Roman diplomacy also seems to have engineered a stabilising balance of power in southern England between the Atrebates along the upper Thames valley and the descendants of Cassivellaunus in Hertfordshire. By far the ablest of the latter was Cunobelinus, who ruled continuously for forty years, steadily encroaching on the Atrebates until he had brought most of southeastern England under his control. After the death of Cunobelinus in AD 40 his two sons Togodumnus and Caractacus showed rather less diplomatic ability, completely over-running the Atrebates, whose leader Verica fled to Rome to ask the emperor for assistance. Verica's appeal catalysed the second and more lasting Roman invasion. In fact, an invasion had already been contemplated some years before, partly as a way of gaining fuller access to Britain's considerable mineral and agricultural wealth and partly to stamp out the Druids, whose religion was providing a focus for the enemies of Rome. The Emperor Gaius had massed troops at Boulogne in AD 39 with the intention of crossing the Channel, but a mutiny dislocated his plans. By the time that Verica arrived in Rome the emperor was Claudius, who needed a military victory to consolidate his reputation. In the spring of AD 43 he ordered four legions to Boulogne, again under the command of Aulus Plautius. These legions were all destined to remain in Britain for many years. They were the 2nd (Legio II Augusta), the 9th (Legio IX Hispana), the 14th (Legio XIV Gemina) and the 20th (Legio XX Valeria).

It was early May when the legions landed at Richborough, on the Kent coast south of Ramsgate, where there was a good natural harbour. After some skirmishes they pushed forward to the River Medway and won a decisive battle with Caractacus and Togodumnus, probably near present-day Rochester. After this victory the army advanced to the Thames and there awaited the arrival of Claudius in person. Caractacus meanwhile escaped to the west, but Togodumnus was killed. Claudius arrived in mid-August and stayed only sixteen days, but in that time he was able to take the city of Camulodunum, now Colchester, which was the capital of the Trinovantes, and he also accepted the surrender of eleven tribal kings. Most of them had been hostile to Caractacus and his brother and were glad to enlist Roman support. Claudius left in early September, leaving Aulus Plautius to continue the campaign, while he himself returned to Rome to enjoy the formal victory celebrations.

The next part of the Roman advance was assisted by existing political alignments in Britain. The aggressive expansion of the Trinovantes had so far alienated rulers like Cogidumnus at Chichester, Prasutagus of the Iceni in Norfolk, Boduocus of the Dobunni in Gloucestershire and Queen Cartimandua of the Brigantes further north that they were prepared to allow Roman troops in their territories. All four of the legions had been concentrated at Colchester to ensure Claudius's victory. Only the 20th remained there, while the others were split in three battle-groups or vexillations and fanned out across southern Britain, making roads and temporary forts or marching camps as they went. The 9th legion was sent northwards and established a base near Peterborough, the 14th headed northwestwards towards Leicester, while the 2nd, under the future Emperor Vespasian, went southwards to fight the Durotriges in Dorset. Aulus Plautius himself returned to Rome in AD 48, but the military advance and consolidation continued under his successors so that, by the middle of the century or shortly after, the 9th legion had reached Lincoln, the 14th Wroxeter in Staffordshire and the 2nd Exeter. The fiercest fighting had been in Dorset and also near the River Severn in what is now Herefordshire and South Wales, where the refugee Caractacus stirred up stiff opposition. All the southern and more fertile half of the country was under Roman control, and the Roman road called the Fosse Way, running between the fortresses of Exeter and Lincoln, can be taken as the dividing line, though not the actual frontier.

The advance against the tribes of Wales was interrupted in AD 60 by the rebellion of the East Anglian Iceni tribe under Boudicca or Boadicea. The rebels defeated the 9th legion and captured Colchester and London while the rest of the Romans were engaged in the west, but they were eventually routed by Suetonius Pallinus somewhere in the south Midlands, probably near Towcester. The following decade was spent in strengthening the existing Roman positions rather than further conquests. To a degree this was the predictable consequence of the rebellion, but the Empire itself, under the Emperor Nero, was going through a troubled time which inhibited military activity on the borderlands. Nero's suicide in AD 68 was followed by the 'Year of the Four Emperors', during which the 14th legion was for a time withdrawn from Britain to support one of the contenders. But after the eventual triumph of Vespasian in AD 69, a policy of expansion was resumed. In a sense it had to resume because the Brigantes, who occupied most of the Pennine region in the north from Derbyshire to North-umberland, had abandoned their Queen Cartimandua who was loyal to Rome in favour of her ex-husband Venutius, who was hostile. By the early 70s the 9th legion had established a new fortress at York, well-placed to attack the heart of Brigantia from the east, and by AD 74 the governor Petillius Cerialis had defeated Venutius and pushed northwestwards across the hills as far as Carlisle. His fierce campaign was not followed by any attempt to conciliate the formerly friendly Brigantes and their continuing unrest made it necessary for the Romans to maintain henceforward a powerful military presence in the north.

After a diversion to over-run the Silures in south Wales, northward expansion was continued under Gnaeus Julius Agricola, appointed governor in AD 78. Agricola is probably the most famous governor of Britain, mainly because of the laudatory biography written by his son-in-law Tacitus. He was certainly an immensely active soldier and in his six years of office mounted six campaigns, which eventually took the Roman army to the edge of the Scottish Highlands. At the end of AD 79 he was in control of all the country south of the Tyne/Solway line where Hadrian's Wall now stands, and building roads to link the east and west coasts. In AD 81 he established a line of forts between the Clyde and Forth estuaries, where the Antonine Wall later ran, and in AD 84, his last year as governor, Agricola defeated the massed Caledonian tribes at a place called Mons Graupius which was probably somewhere north of Aberdeen.

By his conquests Agricola had doubled the area of British territory under Roman control. His most striking monument is still the system of roads across the border country, which was fundamental to control of the north. There are also the earthworks or buried remains of the forts built by his soldiers, from simple and probably temporary enclosures to the elaborate legionary fortress of Inchtuthil, near Dunkeld on Tayside, which was built by, and probably for, the 20th legion. These forts often show signs of innovation in the original arrangement of their ditches and ramparts. At the same time, Agricola did not neglect the southern and more peaceful part of the country; he curtailed abuses in the system of tax collecting and, according to Tacitus, 'pressed forward the construction of temples, farms and town houses'. At Verulamium, now St Albans, an inscription records that the newly built forum or marketplace was dedicated by Agricola in AD 79. In several cases the military establishments vacated by troops moving up to the north were turned into civilian towns, among them Exeter, Cirencester and Gloucester. This was a continuing process and later in the century Wroxeter was adapted in a similar way to become the tribal capital of the Cornovii.

In sharp contrast to the well-documented period of Agricola's term as governor, the forty years after his recall in AD 84 are a blank, with no illuminating historical source, but the general tenor of events in the north of the country is clear. Far from being consolidated by a continuing military presence, Agricola's conquests were gradually given up. Presumably the Emperor Domitian calculated that sufficient had been done to cow the tribes in Scotland. The Inchtuthil fortress was abandoned as early as AD 87, and disturbances elsewhere in the Empire led to the temporary withdrawal of the entire 2nd legion before AD 92, together with some of the auxiliary troops. Although Wales could still be held, the northern frontier was drawn back first to the Forth/Clyde line and ultimately, by about AD 105, to the Tyne/Solway line, so that the whole of Scotland had been given up. Burnt and damaged forts in the Scottish Lowlands show that the withdrawal was accompanied by heavy fighting and this was certainly a time of uncertainty and insecurity. During the decade after AD 105 the three principal army bases in England itself were made stronger. These were the fortresses of the 9th legion at York, the 20th at Chester and the 2nd at Caerleon on Usk in South Wales, all of which had their defences improved by the addition of masonry walls

The building of Hadrian's Wall across the narrowest part of northern England began in AD 121. The large fort at Housesteads attached to the south side of the wall was built soon after this in a move which planted a number of permanent forts on the wall's line. Like most Roman forts, it was laid out on a regular plan. The gates at Housesteads were very massive (and the south gate was further enlarged in the sixteenth century when Housesteads was used as a base by 'Moss-Troopers' or bandits). Along the face of the wall small towers were built at regular intervals. To the left of the south gate can be seen first the commandant's house and then the headquarters' building. Both these and the ranges of barrack-blocks show the signs of several rebuildings. Like all Roman forts, Housesteads had a sophisticated drainage system. There was no natural water on the site but large tanks were built to collect rain. One of the largest is in the southeast corner, immediately adjoining the latrine block. Outside the south gate a small civilian settlement grew up, whose remains, now under turf, cover the hillside below the fort.

This view shows more clearly the outline of the fort at Housesteads, with the north and south gates and the central strip containing the most important buildings – the commandant's house, the headquarters' building, the hospital and the granaries.

with towers. Many of the buildings inside the walls were also reconstructed in stone. Such activity seems to indicate that, despite the heavy fighting in the north, all thoughts of expanding the Empire permanently into Scotland had been laid aside.

Following the death of the Emperor Trajan in AD 117 this cautious attitude was extended across the rest of the Empire. Trajan's successor Hadrian virtually abandoned the idea of military conquest and was more concerned to find safe frontiers, preferably natural boundaries like rivers and mountain ranges. Hadrian's accession in AD 118 coincided with a serious rebellion in northern Britain, which was suppressed by governor Q. Pompeius Falco but served to underline the pressing need for a really efficient security network. When the emperor himself arrived in Britain in AD 122 as part of an extended tour of his western provinces he decided on the building of a permanent frontier between the estuary of the River Tyne and the Solway Firth. Presumably the military were already aware of the superb physical advantages for an engineered frontier on this line. Its northern fringe was everywhere provided with a good outlook, and was defined for miles by an imposing escarpment of volcanic cliffs. Behind this natural barrier the gentler slope of the South Tyne and Irthing valleys permitted easy east-west communication, and was indeed already followed by the Roman road known as the Stanegate.

Hadrian appointed his close friend, A. Platorius Nepos, as governor in AD 122 to realise his decision. Nepos arrived from Germany bringing with him a fresh legion, the 6th (Legio VI Victrix) to reinforce the British garrison. The 6th was soon stationed permanently at York and was presumably intended as a replacement for the 9th legion, whose disappearance from recorded history sometime between AD 108 and AD 130 is still something of a mystery. The traditional explanation is that the 9th was annihilated by the British at a place and time unknown, but it now seems more likely that the legion was withdrawn from Britain intact to Holland and then perhaps sent to Judaea, only to be annihilated in the Jewish rebellion of AD 132.

As soon as he arrived, Nepos set the legions to constructing a permanent wall along Hadrian's chosen frontier. This major undertaking was continued under eight successive governors and was probably finished in about AD 130 under Sextus Julius Severus. The idea of a physical frontier was not wholly new.

Both Domitian and Hadrian had ordered the construction of wooden palisades to mark frontier lines in Germany, with look-out posts and barracks close behind the line to provide reinforcements as required. Hadrian's British wall was altogether stronger and more permanent, and is unique among Roman fortifications for the elaborate nature of its defences. Perhaps this was because there were hostile, or at least unfriendly, tribes on both sides of it – the Brigantes to the south and the Selgovae to the north – so that the wall garrison would be required to operate in both directions, and across a considerable area.

There were several forts at Vindolanda before Hadrian's Wall was built, but they are now buried deep below the later fort and the civil settlement. The garrison during the third and fourth centuries was the 4th cohort of Gauls, a mixed infantry and cavalry regiment originally raised in France. Inside the fort itself, only the foundations of the headquarters are exposed, but much more can be seen of the civil settlement outside the line of the walls.

Cawfields milecastle was built by the 2nd legion. Milecastles were small forts which had a permanent garrison. To the east, the wall itself stretches away, clinging to the top of precipitous crags. Running along behind the line of the wall are the two parallel banks and ditch of the Vallum, which was an original element of Hadrian's elaborate boundary.

Birdoswald belongs to the western section of Hadrian's Wall, which was originally built of turf not stone. Only a few yards to the south a steep escarpment drops down to the valley of the River Irthing. The fort was built to the conventional Roman plan, with an oblong enclosure whose stone walls were pierced by four gateways and reinforced by corner turrets. Birdoswald was constructed astride the turf wall, but in later years the wall was rebuilt in stone and diverted to meet the northern corners of the enclosure, instead of the towers of the side gates. In more recent times, a farmyard was built in the northwest corner of the fort.

As finally built, the barrier was 76 miles long and consisted of six elements. There was first the continuous wall, fronted by a large ditch. Secondly there were milecastles or fortlets spaced evenly along the walls at intervals of one Roman mile and thirdly there were smaller towers or turrets, evenly spaced with two between each pair of milecastles. The fourth element was the garrison forts containing substantial detachments of troops, the fifth was the earthwork known as the *vallum*, running south of the wall and consisting of a wide ditch flanked at some distance on each side by a mound. Lastly there was the Military Way, a later road behind the wall. The relationship of all these elements, both chronological and topographical, is complicated, not least because of the many later alterations. Several modifications were made to the wall itself, even during the first building campaign. The original thickness of 10 feet was reduced to 8 feet in parts of the central section, and a 4-mile length of this narrower wall was added at the eastern extremity to continue the barrier to Wallsend on the Tyne. For the 45 miles west of Birdoswald the wall was at first constructed in turf because there was no suitable local stone, and because the land on the south shore of the Solway Firth offered easy landing for northern invaders a line of towers and small forts was soon extended along the coast from Bowness, where the wall ended, to beyond the present Maryport. The whole of the turf wall was later replaced in stone.

All the building work was carried out by regular legionary troops, a reminder of the fact that these regiments contained skilled craftsmen as well as soldiers. Each legion was allotted a section of the wall, starting from the eastern end where a bridge over the Tyne was constructed at Newcastle (Pons Aelius). These sections were about 5 miles long. One group laid the foundations of the wall and built the turrets, while a second brought the wall itself up to its full height of nearly 40 feet on the outside face. Inscribed stones marked the extent of each section and named the unit responsible for finishing it. A similar division of labour was used for building the turf section of the wall.

At first it was intended that the garrison should be based some distance south of the wall on the line of the Stanegate, where it would be able to make use of some earlier forts like Corbridge (Corstopitum) which had been established during Agricola's campaigns. After only a short time the troops were moved right up to the wall and housed in a series of brand-new buildings. Evidence for this change of policy can be seen at some of these forts, like Chesters, House-steads and Birdoswald which were were either grafted to the south face of the wall or planted across it on top of earlier turrets. None of the troops in these forts belonged to the regular legions and the garrison consisted entirely of auxiliary cavalry and infantry. The total nominal strength of the garrison was rather over 10,000 men, with perhaps a further 1000 to 1500 patrolling along the wall itself. Although regiments had to be withdrawn from various parts of Midland England and Wales to make up the required numbers at the new frontier there was still a considerable army south of the wall. The total strength of the legionary and auxiliary troops in Britain during Hadrian's time has been variously estimated at 42,000 and 55,000.

Hadrian died in AD 138, some eight years after the completion of the wall, and almost immediately the new Emperor Antoninus Pius ordered the army in Britain to push forward once again into Scotland. His governor Lollius Urbicus quickly obtained the necessary military victories, built large numbers of forts in the Scottish lowlands and in AD 142 began building a new wall across Scotland's narrow point between the estuaries of the Forth and Clyde. The Antonine Wall was built entirely of turf, with nineteen forts and several fortlets along its 59-mile length. It is not at all clear why Hadrian's elaborate and immensely expensive wall was so abruptly left behind. Possibly it was to allay the insecurities of the Votadini, a tribe friendly to Rome whose territory on the Northumbrian coast lay north of the wall, but if this was true then the building of the wall had been a remarkably ill-considered piece of work. There can be little doubt that the Antonine Wall was intended as a permanent frontier; though obviously less durable than stone, turf was a perfectly serviceable building material and widely used by the Roman army. All the same, the new frontier did not endure very long. Just over ten years later, some time between AD 154 and AD 158, the garrison was abruptly withdrawn to deal with a rebellion among the Brigantes. Troops returned to the Antonine Wall in AD 159, but were again withdrawn, this time for good, in AD 163. Hadrian's Wall was rehabilitated as the permanent frontier, and it was probably at this time that the turf western part was rebuilt in stone. At first glance the building of the Antonine Wall seems a futile operation, but there are indications that the campaigns in Lowland Scotland did something to stabilise the region and to lessen the threat of a serious invasion.

*W*all (or Letocetum) was a small Romano-British town on Watling Street, the main road from London to the west Midlands. It probably began life as a fort built by the 14th legion shortly after the Roman invasion, but later became a civilian town with a posting station for travellers on official business. The remains of the town lie under the turf but they are extensive and indicate that Letocetum was a place of some importance. An excavation just before the First World War uncovered one of the most complete examples of a Roman town bath-house to be found in Britain, which must have served the needs of townspeople and travellers alike. The remains show the signs of several alterations. Beyond it in this view are the walls of the mansio or guest-house, with its rooms arranged round a small courtyard in the manner of the traditional Roman villa.

*N*orth Leigh is one of nearly a dozen Roman villas and farms in the fertile Oxfordshire valleys of the Glyde and Evenlode, most of them conveniently placed near the road called Akeman Street, which connected the towns which were the tribal capitals of the Dobunni at Cirencester and the Catuvellauni at St Albans. At first the villa was a modest building, but in the third and fourth centuries it was gradually expanded and eventually became a classic example of a Roman courtyard villa. Only two sides of the courtyard are now bare of turf and of these the longer north range incorporates the earliest parts of the villa. At the far end of this range can be seen the complicated foundations of the private bath-house. The shed at the angle of the two ranges shelters a handsome mosaic floor belonging to the great dining room.

All the same, the last decades of the second century seem to have been a fairly turbulent period along the wall, though there is a dearth of documentary information. The assassination of the Emperor Commodus in AD 192 precipitated an imperial civil war in which the governor of Britain, Clodius Albinus, was a contestant. Four years later in AD 196, by which time Septimus Severus was the only other survivor in the power-struggle, Albinus crossed into Gaul with the British army, and was subsequently defeated near Lyons. Meanwhile, northern Britain was invaded once again, Hadrian's Wall damaged and many towns and settlements in the north destroyed.

Severus restored order by degrees. Restoration work on the wall seems to have begun in AD 205 and in AD 208 the emperor arrived in person. For the next three years he conducted a series of rather ineffectual campaigns against the Caledonian tribes from his headquarters at York, where he died in AD 211 to be succeeded by his sons Caracalla and Geta. Caracalla concluded his father's war and then returned to Rome, where one of his first acts was to proclaim that all free-born men and women should be counted as Roman citizens. The effect of this decree in a frontier province like Britain was ultimately considerable. Distinctions between legionary and auxiliary troops were lessened and on the civilian side the improved position of ordinary people in the Roman system enhanced the importance of the towns as legal centres. Settlement was encouraged by allowing soldiers to marry and also to hold land, which inevitably strengthened the bond between serving forces and the locality where they were stationed.

For reasons of political security, the province of Britain was now divided in two, the southern half called Britannia Superior and the northern Britannia Inferior. Only the southern half retained a governor of consular rank and the doings of the praetorian northern governor were of less interest to Roman historians and are consequently less well documented. The 220s seem to have been a period of rebuilding, especially in northern Britain, but the history of the period, especially after 225, becomes increasingly obscure. With the murder of the Emperor Gordian III in AD 244 there opened a period of grave trouble for the Roman Empire in general, and in the forty years between this date and the accession of Diocletian in AD 284 at least fifty-five emperors were proclaimed, many to be murdered almost at once. From these troubles Britain remained

*C*hesters is at present the best example of a cavalry fort visible anywhere within the territory of the Roman Empire. It was probably built in the decade after AD 120 by the 6th Legion and its location, close to a bridging-point on the North Tyne, was highly strategic. In the foreground of this view are the foundations of the south gate and beyond it lie first the barracks and stables and then the central headquarters building. What is now a grass track leads off on the left past the bathhouse down towards the bridge, whose abutments survive.

*P*ortchester Castle began life as a Roman fortress and it is now the only example in northern Europe whose complete circuit of walls stands to full height thanks partly to the repairs carried out in the Middle Ages. The great rectangular enclosure lies on a promontory jutting into Portsmouth harbour. In the second half of the third century the coast of Britain was being raided by Franks and Saxons and a series of new forts was built to deter them. Many of these Saxon Shore forts, of which Portchester is one, were built in the 280s at the instigation of the Emperor Probus. After eight centuries the Roman walls were adapted to serve as the envelope for a Norman castle, of which the main element was the tall square donjon tower or keep, which probably dates from about 1120. Next to the keep are the remains of a small palace built at the very end of the fourteenth century for Richard II. The southeast quarter of the Roman fort became the precinct of a priory of Augustinian canons in 1133 and the handsome Romanesque church probably dates from that time.

relatively immune; the Channel deterred the barbarian armies which swept across Gaul and the reforms of Severus had put the northern frontier on a sound footing and encouraged development elsewhere. But at the same time there was a growing threat from piratical Saxon raiders in the North Sea and along the east coast. By about AD 270 these threats had become acute; there is a steep rise in the number of coin hoards from this time, and such panic burying is usually a good indicator of insecurity. As early as the 220s new coastal forts were built at Reculver in Kent, overlooking the Thames estuary and Brancaster on the Wash. Some time in the mid-century the great triumphal monument at Richborough in Kent, erected to commemorate the landing of Claudius in AD 43, was stripped of its decoration and turned into a watch-tower. A system of ditches encircling the tower was also begun, but soon overtaken by the construction of a stone-walled fortress of advanced design. Similar forts were built elsewhere on the south coast at Dover, Lympne and Porchester and on the east coast at Burgh near Yarmouth, Bradwell in Essex and Walton in Suffolk. Most of them were of a new type, with massive free-standing masonry walls reinforced at intervals by projecting towers, which was probably introduced from the eastern provinces by the Emperor Probus. The same system was being used on the other side of the Channel in the strengthening of existing town walls. Most of these Saxon Shore forts – as they came to be called – were probably complete by AD 286, when Carausius, a prefect of the British fleet specifically appointed to combat piracy, proclaimed himself emperor in defiance of the newly appointed Diocletian.

Although Carausius seems to have been an efficient governor, as well as a popular soldier, his timing was unfortunate. Diocletian proved himself an extremely able emperor and quickly united the rest of the Empire under his control. He realised that the burden of administration was too great for one person and appointed Maximianus as co-emperor, with responsibility for the western provinces. He also instituted the system known as the tetrarchy, whereby each emperor appointed an heir and abdicated in his favour after a set number of years. Maximianus chose Constantius Chlorus and it was he who re-took Britain in AD 296, three years after the murder of Carausius. The effect on the country was immediately beneficial; trade picked up and inflation grew less. There followed a decade of re-organisation in which the civil and military administration were separated and the two British provinces were again divided.

Pevensey was the last to be built of the series of coastal forts under the command of the Count of the Saxon Shore, and probably dates from about AD 330. Its Roman name was Anderida. Pevensey does not have a rectangular plan but, instead, the massive masonry walls follow the outline of what was originally a peninsula rising above the marshes. According to the Anglo-Saxon Chronicle there was a massacre of Britons by invading Saxons at Pevensey in 491, but otherwise nothing is known of the history of the site for six centuries following the Roman withdrawal. After the Norman Conquest in 1066 Count Robert of Mortain made a castle in the southeast corner of the enclosure, and later brought the whole circle of walls back into use. Later owners built a keep, a new inner curtain wall with interval towers and a strong gatehouse tower. As the sea receded and the harbour silted up, Pevensey's importance declined and by Tudor times it was derelict. Another lease of life was given to the defences in the Second World War, when some of the towers were transformed into camouflaged gun-emplacements.

Hadrian's Wall was once more repaired, along with many of the other forts in the north. Constantius stayed in Britain only one year but returned again in AD 306 to oversee a campaign in Scotland. His health was already failing and in 311 he died at York.

The army at once proclaimed his son Constantine as successor; in 312 Constantine left for Gaul and five years later he had become sole ruler of the Roman Empire. The repairs and reforms of Constantius stood Britain in good stead and for the first half of the fourth century the province enjoyed peace and prosperity; some have seen the years before AD 350 as the Golden Age of Roman Britain, but there were signs of trouble to come. The Emperor Constans paid a flying visit in 342, presumably after an incident of some kind, and a short time after this some of the northern forts seem to have been burnt. The raids by sea-borne Saxons continued and probably in the 330s Pevensey was added to the Saxon Shore forts. After about 360 the raids by Picts from Scotland, Scots from Ireland and other raiders intensified. The army in Britain had been utterly weakened by successive withdrawals of troops to fight abroad and in AD 367 a concerted attack by all the hostile groups succeeded in capturing the wall and over-running much of northern England. At the same time the Count of the Saxon Shore, Britain's principal naval commander, was captured and killed. After two lawless years the Emperor Valentinian despatched Count Theodosius with four regiments to put the country in order. He landed at Richborough in AD 368 and by the end of AD 369 had the country in hand once again. Yet another major refurbishment programme of defences and institutions ensued; northern forts were repaired and some sort of non-aggression pact made with northern tribes. More significantly, Theodosius encouraged moves to improve the walls of civilian settlements and may even have stationed contingents of regular troops inside them. This was to be the last constructive large-scale intervention by central government into British affairs.

Theodosius left behind him an ordered country, which endured until 383 when Magnus Maximus, Duke of the Britains, rebelled against central authority. He took most of the British garrison, including the 20th legion, abroad to support his claim to be emperor of the west but was defeated and killed in AD 388. The troops did not return. Virtually the same thing happened in AD 407 when the discontented army rump elected a common soldier named Constantine as an imperial contender. He crossed to Gaul in 408 taking with him all the remaining mobile troops. Despite being recognised by the Emperor Honorius as a suitable governor of the western provinces, Constantine meddled in central politics and was eventually executed in AD 411. Britain was now deprived of regular army protection. In disgust at Constantine's withdrawal the people dismissed his civil servants and in AD 410 the leading citizens addressed a petition for help directly to Honorius. He replied, helplessly, that the towns of Britain should look to their own defences.

There was no immediate collapse. After four hundred years Roman habits of life were ingrained; towns were planned on Roman lines and villas derived from Italian models dotted the countryside. Presumably this way of life continued for several generations on a diminishing scale. There are no contemporary written sources but excavations often reveal evidence of gradual decline and decay. Our picture of Britain in the fifth and sixth centuries comes from later writers like Gildas and Nennius and from the Anglo-Saxon Chronicle. From them we learn of Vortigern inviting the Saxons to settle in southern England probably in about AD 430, and of the ensuing struggles between Britons and Saxons which culminated in the Battle of Badon, some time about AD 500. But facts are hard to come by. The location of Badon is unknown and the identity of the British victor is uncertain, although some maintain he was King Arthur.

A B B E Y S
A N D   P R I O R I E S

emains of mediaeval abbeys and priories can be found in various forms all over England. Some of our most splendid cathedrals were once abbey churches and very often the buildings which once served their monks still survive, though turned to other uses. A substantial number of parish churches also began life as part of an abbey, and it is not particularly unusual to come across private houses converted out of what were originally abbey buildings. These alternative uses followed the dramatic happenings of the early sixteenth century, and in particular the Act of Suppression passed in 1536 at the instigation of King Henry VIII. By this and subsequent acts all monastic foundations in England were shut down, their inhabitants expelled and their lands taken into the hands of the crown. Buildings which could not be made to serve an alternative use were either pulled down or more often merely abandoned. During the next three hundred years they were utterly neglected, valued if at all only as a free source of ready-prepared building materials. Nineteenth-century tastes for the romance of the Middle Ages and for Gothic architecture made the ruins seem of importance once more. There is no space here to chart the complicated evolution of Gothic architecture in England but, as Victorian archaeologists quickly realised, the abbey churches were of crucial importance in the development of the new style. Their builders introduced many new ideas into England – rib vaults at Durham, Purbeck marble shafts at Canterbury, wide traceried windows at Westminster – which were subsequently taken up in other buildings.

For reasons which will soon become clear, many abbeys were built in remote parts of England far from any town or village, and on the whole it is these

In an orchard near this building a stone was found in 1675 inscribed with these words: 'Earl Odda ordered this royal chapel to be built and dedicated in honour of the Holy Trinity for the good of the soul of his brother Elfric, who died in this place. Bishop Ealdric dedicated it on April 12th in the 14th year of Edward, King of the English', i.e., in 1056. Odda's Chapel was later incorporated as part of a timber-framed farmhouse and it was not until 1885 that it was recognised as an important Saxon monument and restored to something like its original appearance.

Muchelney was once a large island in the marshes and water is still never far from the surface. Benedictine monks were established here as early as the seventh century but this early monastery was probably destroyed by the Danes. Muchelney was re-founded in about 950 and survived until the 1530s. The only building of the abbey still standing is the handsome abbot's house which was rebuilt in the decades immediately before the Dissolution. To the right of it are the foundations of the cloister and of the abbey church. At the centre of the abbey is the outline of a small crypt belonging to the first building on the site. The Norman church was of the standard type with a rounded east end, but later in the Middle Ages a rectangular Lady Chapel was added to the east of the high altar.

buildings which are now in the care of English Heritage. Their ruins can be enjoyed merely for the picturesque qualities of their rural settings, but such enjoyment must surely be enhanced by an understanding of the main outlines of monastic life. To this end it may be helpful to give a résumé of the religious history of the monastic heyday in the early Middle Ages in which the various different monastic orders flourished. Perhaps it will be as well to begin with two simple definitions: an abbey is a community of monks governed by an abbot (or a community of nuns by an abbess); a priory is a similar community governed by a prior or prioress. Priories were usually founded as dependants of existing abbeys, whose abbot retained supreme jurisdiction.

The great majority of English abbeys were founded in the 150 years after the arrival of the Norman invaders in 1066, though some were founded considerably earlier. After the final departure of the Romans at the beginning of the fifth century, Christianity suffered a slow decline in the face of unbelieving Saxon invaders. St Augustine arrived in AD 597 to revive the faith and persuaded King Ethelbert to found a monastery at Canterbury in 605 which eventually became the cathedral. The monks at Canterbury were Benedictines, that is to say they followed the rule of daily life and the pattern of regular worship laid down by St Benedict at his monastery of Monte Cassino near Naples. Fundamental to the rule were the three vows of poverty, chastity and obedience. Although these monastic obligations filled the day (Benedict felt that 'idleness is the enemy of the soul') they were not supposed to be particularly rigorous. 'Let all things be done in moderation, on account of the faint-hearted.'

By the seventh century all England had been reconverted and in the eighth century British monks established a reputation for scholarship and art, exemplified in the historical writings of the Venerable Bede and the illuminated Gospels from Lindisfarne in Northumberland. This flowering was cut off during two centuries of uncertainty, and many of the northern monasteries were destroyed in ninth- and tenth-century Danish raids. Towards the end of the tenth century a second revival was instigated by St Dunstan, Abbot of Glastonbury from AD 940 and Archbishop of Canterbury from AD 960. Dunstan introduced the Benedictine rule at Glastonbury and other West Country monasteries, and at the Synod of Winchester in 965 obtained approval for the *Regularis Concordia*, a uniform set of observances for all monasteries in the country. The first fifty years

Two miles from modern Salisbury lies Old Sarum. A new cathedral was begun here soon after the transfer of the see from Sherborne in 1075. During the time of Bishop Herman, a great Romanesque church along continental lines, with a long nave and round apsed ends to the choir and transepts, was built. The extent of this church is marked out on the ground, its eastern parts enclosed by the elaborate extensions made for the most part during the first forty years of the twelfth century under the direction of Bishop Roger.

The massive earthworks at Old Sarum (see previous page) are those of an Iron Age hill fort, whose ramparts and interior were improved and modified to accommodate a mediaeval castle and a cathedral. The castle with its own circle of defences in the centre of the site was altered in the early twelfth century by Bishop Roger in a manner which suggests that it was more comfortable than most castles and probably served as the bishop's palace. Roger died discredited in 1139 and the ensuing poor relations between the clergy and the military, combined with the lack of a convenient water supply, eventually led to the removal of the bishopric to New Sarum or Salisbury in 1219, after which the old settlement slowly declined.

of the eleventh century saw a slow increase in the number of English monasteries so that by the time of the Norman Conquest there were about thirty-five foundations, all Benedictine. Most of the Anglo-Saxon abbeys were probably fairly small, though it is difficult to be certain because so little of this period survives. Muchelney in Somerset is one early foundation where excavation has revealed the outline of early abbey buildings. Deerhurst Priory in Gloucestershire, now a modest parish church, is one of the few survivors of the late Saxon period. Only 200 yards from it is Odda's Chapel, a memorial chapel built by Earl Odda and dedicated in 1056. Still virtually intact after centuries of domestic use, this tiny building underlines the small size of most Saxon places of worship.

With the arrival of the Normans there was an immediate increase in the volume of religious building, and in the scale of the various undertakings. Legend has it that even before the Battle of Hastings Duke William had vowed to build an abbey as a thank-offering if he were victorious, and certainly work began on Battle Abbey soon afterwards. In 1070 the Saxon archbishop, Stigand, was replaced by the Norman Lanfranc, who energetically set about re-founding many of the existing English abbeys. In most cases he replaced the Saxon bishops and abbots with Normans, and often replaced the Saxon monks as well. These new religious leaders began at once to enlarge or completely rebuild the old churches. To some extent this was a natural consequence of a revival of religious enthusiasm, but there is no doubt at all that Lanfranc's re-organisation of the abbeys was as much a part of Norman political strategy as the giving of English lands to Norman noblemen, and it was undoubtedly effective. For the next century it was usual for the leaders of the religious community to be French-speaking, and to have strong ties of loyalty to France.

From the beginning of the century the number of monasteries in Europe as a whole had been increasing steadily, a reflection of the growing importance of religious affairs in daily life. The popularity of Christian institutions was further stimulated by the various crusades or holy wars in the Near East, which led eventually to the creation of the two military orders of the Knights Hospitaller in 1092 and the Knights Templar in 1118. Many of the more devout monks found the traditional Benedictine discipline too lax for the times and Benedictine abbeys too much bound-up with the secular world. Monks in Burgundy felt the problem most acutely and this part of central France saw a series of attempts to

The Benedictine Abbey of Battle was probably the first monastic house founded after the Norman Conquest and stands on the north side of the battlefield, which occupies the foreground in this view. The abbey church was consecrated in 1094, its high altar apparently marking the spot where King Harold was killed. Battle was a wealthy foundation and in consequence many of the original buildings were rebuilt over the centuries in handsome style. One example of this process is the great gatehouse, one of the finest monastic gatehouses in England, which was reconstructed in the 1330s. Battle followed the normal monastic plan, with the monks' quarters laid out round a cloister on the south side of the church. Of the church itself there is nothing now standing, although the outlines of its east end are marked in the grass. On the west side of the cloister was the abbot's house, which has been greatly altered and rebuilt since the Dissolution and is now a private school. On the east side was the dorter, whose tall gable and roofless walls survive.

Castle Acre (see previous page) was a Cluniac priory and directly subservient to the enormously rich and prestigious Abbey of Cluny in France. It was probably founded in about 1090 by William de Warenne, 2nd Earl of Surrey, whose parents had visited Cluny and been immensely impressed by the splendid buildings and the religious life. This view of the abbey buildings is taken from the southwest, looking across the cloister towards the abbey church. Monastic communities were usually equipped with sophisticated water and drainage systems and Castle Acre was no exception. In the foreground is a small stream running under the rere-dorter or latrine block at the end of the dorter. Also straddling the stream are the foundations of a detached kitchen, built in the later fourteenth century to replace the earlier kitchen at the corner of the cloister with its four great piers.

introduce a stricter rule of life. At the beginning of the tenth century Abbot Berno founded Cluny Abbey. The Cluniac order soon spread into Normandy and first appeared in England with the founding of Lewes Priory in 1077 (all Cluniac houses began life as priories, under the control of the mother-house). The Cluniacs always believed that the worship of God demanded offering continuous prayer in fitting splendour and their monasteries became a byword for wealth and opulence. Writing in 1124, St Bernard of Clairvaux observed disdainfully, 'I will not speak of the immense height of their churches, of their immoderate length, of their superfluous breadth, costly polishing and strange designs, which, while they attract the worshipper, hinder the soul's devotion.' Certainly the remains of the English Cluniac house at Castle Acre suggest that the builders took an immense pleasure in elaborate surface decoration.

St Bernard himself was a conspicuous member of a much more successful reforming order, the Cistercians. This order had been established in 1098 by the Englishman Stephen Harding at Cîteaux in Burgundy, as an offshoot of the older Benedictine abbey of Molesme. Within twenty years four more Cistercian houses had sprung up in France, including Clairvaux. The energy of its founders, monastic puritans, established an order that challenged the pre-eminence of the powerful and wealthy Benedictines. Cistercians spread throughout western Europe with extraordinary rapidity. By 1120 the number of their abbeys had increased to twelve and in 1152, when the grand chapter of the order forbade the building of any more houses, there were 340, of which fifty were in England and Wales. From their white cassocks the Cistericans were called the White Monks, setting them apart from the black-clad Benedictines.

All Cistercian abbeys followed as closely as possible the way of life at Cîteaux and their abbots met annually to ensure consistency in what was effectively a monastic federation. No Cisterican abbeys were to be built in towns, but rather in wild and remote places. The buildings themselves were to be of the utmost simplicity, with no sculpture or other decoration, plain glass in the windows and plain fittings. Religious observances were the same as those of the Benedictines, but austerity was the watchword. The first Cistercian house in England was established at Waverley in Surrey in 1128, but the wilder parts of the country in the north and west were much more suitable for a simple and secluded life. Within a very few years the order had established several major

Cluniac abbeys were often distinguished by the elaboration of their architecture. The west front of Castle Acre is a very fine example of twelfth-century ornament. Both the end-wall of the nave and the remains of the towers which flanked it have several tiers of blind and interlacing arcades. Some of this decoration was destroyed in the fifteenth century when the great west window was inserted. Immediately next to the church is the prior's lodging, which originally consisted of a single simple block. By the beginning of the sixteenth century the prior had taken over the whole of the west side of the cloister for the use of himself and his guests, extending and elaborating the old building.

*R*ievaulx, founded in
the narrow valley of
the River Rye in 1131,
was the first major
monastery built in
Britain by the
Cistercians, and there is
more left standing than at
any other Cistercian
abbey in England except
Fountains. The
spaciousness of the
buildings shows the size
and wealth of the
establishment. The first
abbey church was
completed in the twelfth
century, but after 1225
the entire east end was
richly rebuilt and this
later work survives
almost intact. Next to the
south transept can be seen
the remains of the
elaborate round-ended
chapter house and then
the walls of the monks'
quarters, of which the
great refectory block with
its pointed windows is
most conspicuous.

Buildwas lies in a loop of the River Severn, with its cloister placed between the church and the river on the north side, instead of the customary south. It was a Savignac foundation, established in 1135. The Savignacs merged with the Cistercians twelve years later and Buildwas conforms to the normal Cistercian arrangements, with buildings which were simple, but up-to-the-minute in architectural fashions, as witness the pointed arches of the nave arcade. In this view the foundations of the pulpitum screen dividing the nave can be seen very clearly.

houses in Yorkshire and along the Welsh Marches. Among them were the great monasteries of Rievaulx (1131) and Fountains (1132) which became the pre-eminent Cistercian foundations in Britain. One reason for the rapid growth of the Cistercian order was that endowing a Cistercian monastery was fairly easy. Wealthy patrons could afford to be generous with grants of undeveloped land.

Manual work was a central part of Cistercian discipline, indeed the motto of the order was 'labour is prayer', but at the same time it was essential that the daily services of the church should be observed. The solution was a system whereby the inhabitants of each abbey were divided into monks and lay-brothers, or *conversi*. The former were literate and conducted the services prescribed by the rule, the latter were full-time manual labourers who worked on the abbey lands and in the mills and workshops. The two sorts were distinct and lived in different parts of the precinct. During the twelfth and thirteenth centuries the *conversi* often considerably outnumbered the monks; at Rievaulx in the time of Abbot Ailred (1147–1167) there were 140 monks and 600 *conversi* and smaller monasteries reflected these proportions in lesser numbers. This proved an extremely efficient arrangement and enabled the Cistercians to bring large areas of hitherto wild country under cultivation. They soon showed that the uplands in which they settled were particularly suitable for sheep-rearing, and immense profits accrued to the monks from the sale and export of wool. In time this wealth led the Cistercians into the same ostentation as the Benedictines before them.

In the face of temptation from material wealth or political influence only one order, the Carthusians, managed to preserve their integrity. The order was founded in 1084 by St Bruno, and the first house was at Grande Chartreuse near Grenoble. Carthusians lived in solitude and silence. Their monasteries were quite unlike the rest and consisted of a series of small individual houses grouped round a cloister with only a modest church. 'Their dress is meaner and poorer than that of other monks, so short and scanty and so rough that the very sight affrights one. They wear coarse hair shirts next the skin, fast almost perpetually, eat only bean bread whether sick or well, never touch flesh, their constant occupation is reading, praying and hard labour.' Carthusians first appeared in England in 1178, when King Henry II founded a house at Witham on the Wiltshire/Somerset border as a penance for the murder of Thomas à Becket. The number of monks in each house was strictly limited to twelve, with eighteen lay

*R*oche was founded in 1147. The plan of the great church follows the standard Cistercian arrangement, with an aisled nave, transepts and a straight-ended chancel. Only the lowest parts of the nave walls and the columns of the eight-bay arcades survive, but the transept walls are still almost full-height. Their historical importance lies in the fact that they were built just as the heavy round-arched Romanesque style was being replaced by the pointed arches of the Gothic style, probably in about 1170. The other buildings of the abbey follow a textbook arrangement, with the monks' living rooms round the great cloister and the abbot's lodgings and infirmary beyond the stream which provided fresh water and drainage. The valley was landscaped by Capability Brown in the eighteenth century as part of the grounds of nearby Sandbeck Park.

brothers to look after their material wants. There was no incentive for expansion and the number of Carthusian houses increased only slowly, with two more in the next 150 years. But the evident integrity of the Carthusians helped them retain popular respect and there were eventually nine houses in England, of which Mount Grace in Yorkshire founded in 1398 by Thomas Holland, Duke of Surrey, is by far the best preserved.

For decades before the Norman Conquest there had been another international family of regular clergy, the secular canons. A secular canon was a priest not under a vow nor living according to a rule, and many of the larger churches and cathedrals were served by communities of these canons, distinct from the individual priests serving parish churches, or monks under Benedictine vows. In some of the major ecclesiastical centres like Canterbury reforming British bishops replaced the canons with monks; the alternative was to impose a new rule. At the Lateran Council of 1059 reform was urged on all such communities, along the lines of a code of conduct laid down in the fifth century by St Augustine of Hippo. Those communities where the new rule was accepted were known as Augustinian, or regular canons, as distinct from unreformed secular canons. The first community to submit to the new rule in England was the Priory of St Botolph, Colchester, in 1103. With some notable exceptions, Augustinian priories were seldom of any great size. Many were founded in conjunction with a parish church and were closely bound-up with local life. Partly for this reason, they retained general popularity well into the fourteenth century and many of their buildings still survive in parish use.

Besides the Augustinians there were several other orders of canons, including those of Arrouaise near Bapaume, Ste. Victoire in Paris, the Premonstratensians from Premontre near Laon and the English Gilbertines. The Premonstratensians, or white canons, who arrived in Britain in the 1140s consciously imitated the Cistercians; they had a liking for rural sites and a federal system linking all the houses. They were fairly successful, and in the first hundred years in this country established thirty-one abbeys in England, including Bayham in Sussex (1208) and Titchfield in Hampshire (1232), but Titchfield was almost the last foundation and by the mid-thirteenth century the Premonstratensian expansion was over. The Gilbertines were unusual in being the only post-conquest monastic order to originate in England, and the only one in which

O f the gatehouse to the precinct of Roche Abbey only the ground floor survives.

it was possible to unite women and men in the same foundation. Gilbert was the priest of Sempringham in Lincolnshire. His first house was set up there in 1131, with the nuns under the Benedictine rule, the monks under Augustinian and the lay brothers and sisters under Cistercian. The order achieved a modest success, principally in Lincolnshire and the surrounding counties.

By about 1200 much of the impact of the monasteries was spent. Many of them had grown into rich and powerful components of the establishment, but were less commonly the focus of religious enthusiasm. Indeed the wealth of the monasteries was beginning to be criticised and the energy of the Cistercian farmers rebounded on them. At the same time, the fundamentals of religious faith were being subjected to critical scrutiny in the new universities and heretical sects like the Albigensians seemed to threaten traditional doctrine. The need to confront these difficulties brought into being the preaching orders or friars, notably the Dominicans or Black Friars from Spain and the Franciscans or Grey Friars from Assisi in northern Italy. These new mendicant orders, so-called because they were supposed to make their living from begging, were committed to the missionary role of preaching the word of God, and by the mid-thirteenth century they were firmly established in England with houses in the main towns and universities, despite considerable opposition from the older orders.

In the three centuries between the arrival of the friars and the Dissolution, English monasteries continued to function and often to flourish, despite various setbacks. The Statute of Mortmain passed in 1279 made it more difficult for monasteries to acquire land; the Black Death of 1349 and the subsequent plagues of 1361 and 1368 hugely reduced the number of monks and lay-brothers, making it more difficult to farm the lands already in hand. War with France was almost continuous between 1336 and 1453 and in 1414 the Act for the Suppression of Alien Priories forced many houses to sever their links with French mother-houses and also to pay a substantial fine to become 'denizens' of England. But although some houses never really recovered after the Black Death, others were well able to find the money for expensive new buildings, and the sixteenth century in particular saw the construction of some splendid new ranges of abbots' lodgings.

Several of the smaller monasteries were closed in the sixteenth century, by Cardinal Wolsey among others, so that their assets could be re-distributed to

Like Buildwas in Shropshire, Byland Abbey was a Savignac foundation which later merged with the Cistercians. The church was completed in 1225 and its handsome west wall still survives, with elegant columnar decoration and the lower half of a great rose window. All three doorways were originally covered by a porch or galilee, whose foundation wall and roof supports can still be seen. Like many Cistercian monasteries in the north, Byland drew its wealth from sheep-farming, which was overseen by the conversi or lay brothers. They were housed in the west range of the cloister, which had its own direct access into the western part of the church.

other, principally educational, purposes. These and the previous restrictive measures had been taken with the approval of the Pope, but after the death of Wolsey in 1529 King Henry, baulked by Rome of his divorce from Catherine of Aragon, broke England from papal control by a series of acts of parliament, notably the Act of Supremacy (1534) which made Henry head of the church. During 1535 all monasteries were inspected and their income assessed by the Vicar General Thomas Cromwell, or his agents, in a survey known as the *Valor Ecclesiasticus*. In 1536 the Act of Suppression forced the closure of all houses with fewer than twelve inmates and an annual income of less than £200 and ordered the confiscation of their assets. Larger foundations were subjected to similarly hostile pressure and in 1539 a further act ensured that all religious houses, once closed, would come into the hands of the crown. Not all their buildings were demolished. Twelve old cathedrals and five new ones, together with over one hundred abbey churches, continued in use for worship while many others were converted for secular purposes. At Titchfield and at Mottisfont in Hampshire, for example, the nave was turned into a mansion, at Lacock in Wiltshire and Newstead in Nottinghamshire the same fate befel the abbey cloister, while at Muchelney and Forde in the West Country the abbot's lodging was adapted with ease for a new secular occupant.

The routine of life in the monasteries varied according to the different orders, but some features were constant. Central to every foundation was the daily round of religious services, from matins and lauds in the small hours of the morning, through prime, terce, sext and none to vespers and compline in the early evening. Other tasks were distributed in the daily morning meeting in the chapter house. The main meal was served in the late morning and on most days a less substantial meal called supper was served in the late afternoon. In Cistercian abbeys the *conversi* had a slightly different regime, rising at dawn, and with fewer church services to allow more time in the fields or workshops.

All the regular functions of the abbey were under the immediate supervision of individual monks or nuns called obedientiaries who were responsible to the abbot or abbess. These obedientiaries usually included the precentor responsible for the arrangement of the church services including the music, the sacristan who cared for the fittings of the church and the vestments, the cellarer who had charge of the various food stores and oversaw the food supplies, the kitchener in the

*C*leeve was a fairly modest Cistercian abbey founded towards the end of the twelfth century. Little remains of the church except low foundations but the east and south sides of the cloister are nearly intact. The east range containing the monks' dormitory dates from the thirteenth century. The south range was rebuilt late in the fifteenth century and has a first-floor frater or dining room with a magnificent ornamental timber roof. From the outside the frater is marked by large traceried windows.

kitchen, the fraterer or refectorian who oversaw the laying of tables and serving of food, the chamberlain in charge of the household arrangements in other parts of the abbey, the infirmarian, the hospitaller or guest-master and the master of the novices. Only the larger foundations would have a full complement of these officers, but even at the smallest houses the same functions were enjoined by the rule and had to be carried out.

Whatever the order, virtually all abbeys and priories built after the Norman Conquest followed the same general arrangement, in which the two main elements were the church, usually cruciform, and a rectangular cloister with the living accommodation of the monks or nuns grouped round it. In addition, there was often a separate guest house, an infirmary, and an outer courtyard with the wash-house, bake-house, brew-house and other necessary facilities. The whole precinct was often enclosed by a wall and entered by a gate-house. The only non-conforming order was the Carthusian, where the cloister was surrounded by the cells of individual monks and not by communal facilities.

The interior of the church was divided into distinct sections, and often the divisions were made by solid partitions whose foundations are still visible. In the sanctuary or presbytery that occupied three or four bays of the choir or eastern arm, stood the high altar, usually raised on steps. In those foundations where there was a shrine containing the remains of a saint or other holy relic it was usually placed east of the high altar. West of the presbytery were the seats for the monks, arranged facing one another in collegiate fashion and often extending south of the transepts and crossing and into the nave. The monks' choir was closed at the western end by a screen known as the pulpitum, from which the epistle and gospel were read on certain days. Two bays west of the pulpitum was the rood screen, surmounted by the great cross and extended across the aisles on either side by lower parclose screens. Thus the whole of the eastern parts of abbey churches was reserved solely for the use of the monks or nuns. The transepts provided space for small chapels and in addition the south transept usually contained an entrance from the cloister and the north transept a door to the monks' cemetery. That part of the nave west of the rood screen was really an enormous vestibule to the choir and used for processions and further altars. In Cistercian churches it was used by the *conversi* for their separate services, and in cathedrals and some other abbeys for public services.

Hailes was one of the last Cistercian abbeys in England, founded in 1245 by Richard of Cornwall as a thanks offering after his rescue from shipwreck. Richard was the king's brother and Hailes was a wealthy foundation with splendid buildings. In 1270 it was presented with a phial of the Holy Blood, which made the abbey one of the more notable pilgrimage centres of mediaeval England. To house this relic the original straight east end of the church was rebuilt and extended in the form known as a chevet, with a coronet of radiating chapels. After the Dissolution the west range of the cloister (in the foreground here) was converted into a private house, but later demolished.

Although this pattern remained basically unchanged until the Dissolution it was frequently modified and appeared in a number of different guises. Norman churches in England were always longer than their French counterparts, but early Norman choirs were fairly short and usually ended in a semi-circular apse. The Cistercians at first insisted that the east ends of their churches should be straight, with no elaboration; though some of their later buildings abandoned this form, the straight end remained a characteristic of Cistercian churches and was imitated across England in churches belonging to other orders. Towards the end of the eleventh century there was an increasing need for numbers of smaller chapels, mostly to serve as private chantries where special masses were said for the souls of benefactors. The Cistercian abbey at Byland in Yorkshire (1177) has a row of them along the east end of the choir, but after the rebuilding of the eastern parts of Canterbury Cathedral between 1174 and 1184, with the splendid new shrine of Thomas à Becket, the practice of making an altogether more elaborate east end was widely adopted. There was something of a vogue for new shrines in the thirteenth century and since the whole point of such things was that visitors should have access to view the relics and to pray at the shrine altar it was necessary to make suitable provision for them, with an ambulatory leading behind the high altar. One of the few Cistercian examples can be seen at Hailes Abbey, which was presented in 1270 with a phial of the Holy Blood, and where the whole east end was reconstructed with a polygonal east end probably based on Westminster Abbey. In the second half of the thirteenth and the fourteenth century the increasing importance placed on the worship of the Virgin Mary led to the building of new lady chapels, usually at the east end of the choir. Cistercians alone, whose churches were all dedicated to the Virgin, did not need a separate altar for her veneration.

There were other reasons for replacing parts of monastic churches. It should be borne in mind that building operations at new abbeys always started with the east and more important parts of the church. The construction and finishing of the rest might take decades and by the time the whole was finished the original east end might be unsatisfactory. For one thing, architectural fashions would have changed. Most monasteries were founded in the late twelfth and early thirteenth centuries, a transitional period of English architecture, when pointed arches were replacing round ones, and there must have been great temptation in

*U*nlike the monks of other orders, Carthusians lived silent and solitary lives, isolated in their cells and meeting only for worship, and for conversation once a week. Mount Grace in Yorkshire, founded in 1398, is the best-preserved Carthusian monastery in England. Round the far cloister are arranged the cells, each with its own small garden. The church itself was a modest affair and stands between the monks' cloister and the outer enclosure containing the kitchen and other necessary buildings.

the wealthier abbeys to keep up with the times. Another reason for rebuilding was to gain more space; this was certainly one of the motives behind the splendid enlargement of the choir at Rievaulx begun in 1225. And in some cases there were probably sound structural reasons for reconstructing an old building.

The domestic accommodation surrounding the cloister also followed a standard arrangement, as far as the lie of the ground would allow. Whenever possible, the cloister was placed on the south side of the church where it would get the most sun. This was the best that could be done to adapt an open courtyard – which derived ultimately from classical Roman villas – to the chilly northern climate. The cloister was the centre of the monks' lives; within these covered walks the brothers studied and copied manuscripts. In later years the openings to the central courtyard were provided with elaborate tracery and glazed in.

The eastern range of cloister buildings was two storeys high. At the end nearest the church was usually the chapter house, which often ran through both storeys. Used for the daily morning meetings of the whole community, the chapter house was second only to the church in importance and was often richly decorated inside. Early chapter houses were usually rectangular, and the Cistercians always retained this shape, but in later years more elaborate forms were sometimes preferred. Beyond the chapter house the ground floor was occupied by a series of smaller rooms which included the *locutorium* where conversation was permitted and the *calefactorium* or warming house, which was the only place where a fire was allowed, other than the kitchen. The whole upper floor of this eastern range was given over to the dorter or monks' dormitory, originally open from end to end and with a stair opening giving directly into the transept of the church so that the monks could reach the night services by the shortest route. Attached to the dorter at the other end, or at right-angles, was the *neccessarium* or rere-dorter, containing the privies. These were often elaborate. Abbeys were planned from the start with an eye to water-supply and drainage; water was often piped into the kitchen and cloister and the rere-dorter was usually flushed by a running stream, which dictated its location.

The south side of the cloister, farthest from the church, was mostly taken up by the monks' dining room called the frater or *refectorium* and somewhere near the entrance would be a *lavaterium* or washing place for the use of the monks before meals. The frater itself was arranged much like an ordinary nobleman's

Titchfield Abbey was a Premonstratensian monastery founded in 1232. The history of the abbey was uneventful, and it survived until 1537. After the Dissolution, Titchfield suffered the fate of many religious buildings. It came into the hands of Thomas Wriothesley who employed a master-mason called Thomas Bertie to transform the nave of the abbey church into a mansion called Palace House. The centre of the old nave was removed altogether and replaced by a great stone gatehouse, which was the principal feature of the new mansion. The greater part of this house was itself destroyed in 1781, leaving only the gatehouse, and the remains have been tidied up to reveal the abbey foundations.

hall of the period, with a high table at the end farthest from the door and doors leading to the serving rooms at the other. The only constant difference was the reader's pulpit, usually in the south wall, from which a devotional text was read during meals. The kitchen itself usually stood behind the frater to the southwest, to keep cooking smells as far from the church as possible, and also to minimise the risk of fire. The two-storied building on the west side of the cloister was usually the *cellarium* or great storehouse and between the *cellarium* and the nave of the church there was commonly the passage known as the outer parlour, which linked the enclosed world of the cloister with the outer courtyard and the outside world. In later centuries, when it had become usual for the abbot to live apart from the monks, it became common practice to convert part of this western range into the abbot's lodgings. In Cistercian houses the presence of the *conversi* sometimes entailed a slightly different arrangement. The lay-brothers usually occupied the whole of the western range, which contained a separate dorter and frater. The frater of the monks was therefore raised up on an undercroft which served as a storage cellar and was normally set at right-angles to the usual building line to allow the insertion of a larger kitchen at the southwestern corner, which could provide for both parts of the community.

Besides the main cloister there were often other enclosures, at least in the larger abbeys. Most of them had an outer courtyard containing not only workshops and outbuildings but also housing for travellers, which might be elaborate. The secluded area to the east of the main cloister was the most favoured location for the infirmary, where sick and elderly monks were looked after. In consideration of their poor health they were permitted meals containing meat, served in a separate eating room called the *misericordia*, and it was a frequent criticism of monasteries in their later years that an increasing number of monks ate too regularly in the *misericordia*. Although in this and other respects the daily life in English monasteries and nunneries became more sophisticated, with a greater emphasis on physical comfort and the needs of the individual which reflected secular developments, the basic arrangements of the cloister changed very little. At Cleeve Abbey in Somerset, which was founded in 1198, the buildings round the cloister were reconstructed in the early sixteenth century by William Dovell, the last abbot, with only the smallest variations from the traditional plan.

C A S T L E S
A N D   F O R T R E S S E S

 astles epitomise the Middle Ages better than any other type of building. Their existence is a monument to the feudal system which underlay mediaeval society. Most of them were built to serve some specific political or military purpose, their defences reflect the currents of thought about military design in Europe and the accommodation they provide illustrates the steady improvement in standards of comfort from the eleventh century to the sixteenth. In popular imagination the castle is usually a gaunt ivy-clad ruin, whose crumbling walls dominate the surrounding countryside. There are certainly ruins enough to satisfy anyone's romantic sensibilities, but most castles repay a more detailed and intellectual scrutiny of their pedigree. Very few of them were built all at once; instead the original strongholds were adapted and improved over the centuries, with the result that most of them are a complicated patchwork. One extreme example is Pevensey Castle in Sussex, which began life as a Roman shore fort, built in about AD 330 to deter Saxon sea-raiders. It was adapted to form the outer wall of a new Norman castle in about 1100 and eventually, after centuries of neglect, was turned into a camouflaged gun battery in the 1940s, with concrete bunkers embedded in the Roman and mediaeval walls.

Although parts of the wall of Pevensey have survived for 2000 years, there is not much left of the domestic buildings which once stood inside them. The same is true of many other castles, which now seem mere empty shells. But it is important to remember that most castles were not only strongholds but also the principal residences of members of the aristocracy. Their military and domestic functions developed side by side in the early Middle Ages, but became increasingly incompatible until, in the first decades of the sixteenth century, they diverged. Thenceforward military and domestic buildings were distinct. Deal Castle, Walmer Castle and the other seashore forts built by Henry VIII were artillery fortresses and nothing more.

The castle, as we understand it, was probably introduced into England at the Norman Conquest in 1066. There is a good deal of dispute about whether the Saxons had castles and what they might have been like, but facts are hard to come by. Certainly the Saxons had their fortified towns and villages called *burghs*, there is some evidence of the existence of fortified Saxon manor houses, and the Anglo-Saxon Chronicle mentions castle-building in Wales just before the Conquest. But these castles were apparently built by 'foreigners', probably friends of Edward the Confessor who spent much of his early life in France, and there were not many of them. On the whole it seems that Saxon fortifications were primarily for communal defence against raiders and casual marauders.

With the arrival of the Normans matters changed completely. Duke William's companions in his victory were rewarded with very substantial grants of land, on the understanding that they would subdue their new tenants. They accomplished this by building strongholds in towns and at other strategic points, whose principal function was not to defend the local population, but to keep them in order. Norman society was more turbulent and individualistic than Saxon, and in that society the castle was already established as a vital element. It was a strong point where the lord kept a grip on his lands, the mustering point where troops might gather, the centre where taxes and other dues might be paid, and not least a symbol of overlordship. In the feudal system of the Middle Ages, which bound serfs to their lords and their lords to the king, the castle was a constant reminder of the delegated royal power.

Immediately after landing, the conqueror built a fort at Pevensey, probably in the Roman walls, and following the victory at Hastings the invaders spread rapidly through the country, building castles as they went. Sometimes they were able to make use of existing fortifications, as at Thetford in Norfolk and Old Sarum in Wiltshire where Iron Age hillforts were turned to good account, but most of these castles were newly built. There is considerable variety in the arrangement of these first Norman castles but they can be grouped into two main types: the ringwork and the motte and bailey. Ringworks were earth banks

Launceston in Cornwall offers one of the more spectacular examples of an early Norman motte. The steep natural hill was further heightened by Count Robert of Mortain, newly created Earl of Cornwall, and fortified with a timber wall by 1086. The motte was a place of last resort and the living quarters were always in the bailey below. For some reason unknown Launceston seems to have kept its wooden walls for well over a century, but at some time after 1216 the top of the motte was crowned with a massive ring-wall or shell keep. By this date the idea of having a strong keep for passive defence was already old-fashioned and perhaps for this reason a taller tower was built inside the first a short time later. This arrangement made Launceston a more effective fighting machine. Access to the keep was by a stair outside the mound, itself roofed-over and fortified.

Berkhamsted Castle demonstrates, almost better than anywhere else, the standard arrangement of an early Norman motte and bailey castle. The exact date for the first building here is not known, but it probably went up within thirty years of the Norman Conquest. The remains consist of an outer and an inner moat surrounding the large area of the bailey. Tucked in one corner of the bailey is the motte or mount, about 45 feet high, which was originally finished with a circular stockade. Both this and the wall of the bailey were rebuilt in stone in the twelfth century.

topped by a stockade and encircled by an external ditch. Motte and bailey castles comprised an earth mount (or motte) with stockade and ditch combined with an enclosure like a ringwork. The ringwork was the simpler form and in many places was probably the first built, but the motte made a more effective show. More than 700 castles with mottes and 200 ringworks are known and the great majority date from the thirty years after 1066. None survives in anything like its original condition but their appearance can be judged from the illustrations in the Bayeux Tapestry and from the remains at places like Launceston in Cornwall and Berkhamsted in Hertfordshire, where the original timber walls were later replaced in stone.

Although the motte and bailey castles were extremely effective, the wooden parts of their defences were subject to decay and both they and the wooden buildings within the walls were vulnerable to fire. In the twelfth century there was a general rebuilding of these early walls in durable and fireproof materials. There are a few examples of stone-built castles from the early years of the Conquest, notably the Tower of London, where work on the building of the quadrangular White Tower began in 1070. This was a structure of great symbolic importance, the palace of the conqueror in the capital city. The massive scale and decorative treatment of its stone walls immediately distinguished the Tower as a centre of power. Other early stone castles were built at Colchester, Ludlow, Rochester and Richmond in Yorkshire and they were the forerunners of the next stage of development.

At many places the old motte was replaced by a stone tower known as a keep or donjon. These towers were usually built directly on the ground, not on the mottes whose unconsolidated earth might form an unstable foundation. Many of them still survive and they range from the relatively simple towers at Portchester (1120s) and Wolvesey Palace in Winchester (1138) to the immensely strong keep at Kenilworth with its solid corner towers and the elaborate structures at Rochester, Castle Headingham, Castle Rising and Norwich. All tower keeps had features in common: immensely thick walls, virtually no windows and an entrance at first-floor level reached through a 'fore-building'. An alternative to the donjon was the 'shell-keep', where the original timber palisade on top of the motte was replaced by a stone enclosure. Among surviving shell keeps are those at Launceston and Restormel in Cornwall, Carisbrooke on

In 1086 Castle Acre belonged to William de Warenne, one of King William's most powerful and trusted supporters, who was later created Earl of Surrey. The castle, probably begun in the 1070s, was long thought to be a typical example of the traditional early Norman type with a tall earth motte and an outer bailey, but recent excavations revealed a different history. At first a large building with elaborate accommodation, which was clearly more of a mansion than a fortress, was constructed on the old land surface. Political unrest after 1120 led the second earl to set about turning this mansion into a keep by stripping out the roofs and floors, blocking the windows, raising the walls and surrounding the keep with earthworks so that the original ground floor of the building became a partially buried basement. The wooden fence round the old building was also replaced by a massive stone wall. In the event, there was a change of plan and part of the mansion was completely demolished to give a much smaller keep. This view shows very clearly the foundations of the two halves of the old mansion.

the Isle of Wight and Arundel in Sussex. Shell-keeps were doubtless as effective as donjons, but they do not have the same presence. In most cases the restricted living accommodation within the keep would have been supplemented by buildings in the bailey.

In the first decades of the twelfth century King Henry I tightened royal control over castle-building, but during the unhappy years of the civil war between King Stephen and Queen Matilda, known as the Anarchy, many unlicensed or 'adulterine' castles sprang up, most only to be demolished after the accession of Henry II in 1153. By one estimate there were as many as 350 of these short-lived forts. The second half of the century saw the re-assertion of royal control. This limited the building of new castles but not the improvement of existing ones and it was probably in this period that the outer walls of many castles were rebuilt in stone. Both Henry II and his French rival Philip Augustus were keenly interested in castle design, and their reigns saw several attempts to improve the keep as a fighting machine. At Gisors in Normandy (1160), Orford in Suffolk (1170), Conisbrough in Yorkshire (1180) and Pembroke, South Wales (1200) the traditional rectangular form was abandoned in favour of an essentially cylindrical shape, which eliminated vulnerable corners and served much better to deflect missiles. On the other hand, it proved difficult to adapt these cylindrical keeps to provide comfortable domestic spaces. Where the residential function of a castle was important there was a strong argument for retaining the traditional rectangular plan which gave a lot more usable space. Henry II's great keep at Dover, begun in the same year as Orford, combined a thoroughly conventional appearance and a high level of domestic comfort with separate suites of rooms and a piped water supply.

Both English and French castle-builders were influenced by the military techniques which they encountered in the Near East during the various crusades. The cylindrical keeps of the late twelfth century were probably a distant reflection of crusader practice, which favoured round and 'D'-shaped towers. In these holy wars the building and beseiging of castles was brought to a high level of sophistication, which owed a great deal to the example of the other side. The improvements are epitomised in crusader castles like Belvoir (or Kaukab-al-Hawa), rebuilt by the Knights Hospitallers in 1168–1188 with two concentric walls, and by the early twelfth century Krak des Chevaliers in Syria, which was

sited on a huge natural mound with interval towers along its walls. After the end of the arduous third crusade, returning soldiers put the innovations they had seen in the Holy Land to good use. Henceforward many walls and towers were given splayed bases and existing arrow-slits were supplemented by machicolations at the wall-head to enable missiles and other deterrents to be dropped onto attackers. Better use was made of cliffs and other natural features, with a preference for tall, virtually inaccessible headlands which put beseigers with their various forms of catapult at a disadvantage. Beeston Castle in Cheshire, built in 1225 on a rocky inland promontory, was the product of this way of thinking. There was no keep and the defences consisted only of walls across the neck of the promontory and an impressive ditch cut 30 feet deep into solid rock. But by far the most important development was the use of interval towers spaced along the main wall and projecting from it. Such towers made it possible to rake the outer face of the walls with fire. The inner ring of walls at Dover, built in the 1180s at the same time as the keep, had fourteen such towers. It was one of the earliest English examples of the type, which was soon followed at the other royal castles at Windsor and the Tower of London.

In the early thirteenth century a few castles were built with defences consisting only of a fortified outer wall, and with no keep. One of the best examples is Framlingham in Suffolk, rebuilt between 1190 and 1210. There was much in these walls with interval towers which recalled Roman examples, but although the Romans had managed perfectly well by concentrating all their defences at the perimeter, twelfth- and thirteenth-century castle-builders in Europe clung to the idea of a central citadel. This can be seen very clearly at Chateau Gaillard, built by King Richard I between 1196 and 1198 in a stunning position high above the River Seine. Its defences were the last word in modernity, with outworks protecting the entrance, concentric walls studded with cylindrical towers and a keep at the centre. There could be no clearer indication of the symbolic importance of an innermost stronghold. In those English castles where a keep already existed it was usually allowed to remain untouched, while the surrounding defences were improved.

One of the best places to see the immediate impact of crusader practice is at Dover, where Henry II's keep and inner wall were strengthened in 1204–1215 during the reign of King John by the addition of an outer curtain wall. The most

Pevensey began life in the fourth century as a Roman coastal fortress. Duke William gave Pevensey to his half-brother Robert of Mortain after the Norman Conquest and it was probably he who built a new stone castle in one corner of the Roman fort.

The most famous castle in England, the Tower (see previous page) stands by the river guarding the eastern side of the old City of London. At the centre is the White Tower, built by William the Conqueror in about 1080. It is larger, earlier in date and more ornamental than most other stone keeps. The reason is simply that William I intended the building to be a palace as well as a stronghold – the visible centre of the feudal system which kept him in power. Encircling the keep are two rings of massive walls with towers at irregular intervals. The inner wall was largely built by Richard I (1189–1199) and Henry II (1216–1272); the outer wall by Edward I (1272–1307). Both have been rebuilt and repaired many times but the basic arrangement has not changed. The Tower of London is in the care of the Department of the Environment.

noticeable difference between them is the shape of the interval towers, the early rectangular type giving way to a 'D' shape, with the rounded surface outwards. In 1216 Dover was beseiged by King Louis of France and nearly taken because of the poor siting of the gate on the north side of the curtain which was overlooked by an area of high ground. When it came to refurbishing the castle in the 1220s the old gate was blocked up and a much stronger one made on the west side, where the ground falls steeply towards the town. Entrance was by way of a very substantial tower, known as the Constable's Tower, which was large enough to contain a decent set of apartments for the chief officer of the castle. This improvement was prophetic; while the detached keep steadily declined in importance during the thirteenth century, the prominent, strongly fortified gatehouse became increasingly common.

From a purely military point of view, the apogee of British castle-building was reached in the second half of the thirteenth century. The best examples are in Wales, but their influence can also be seen in England, particularly along the Welsh border. The earliest of these military masterpieces is Caerphilly in South Wales, built by Gilbert de Clare, Earl of Gloucester, between 1266 and 1277. Caerphilly has two massive concentric walls and particular attention was paid to the main approach, defended by an elaborate barbican which doubled as a dam holding back the great lake encircling the castle. Directly descended from Caerphilly but much better known is the group of castles erected in North Wales at the cost of King Edward I as part of his campaign to subdue the Welsh. The group comprises Flint and Rhuddlan (1277), Conwy, Caernarfon and Harlech (1283) and Beaumaris (1295). In all of them the principal defence was the great outer wall reinforced by towers, while Caernarfon, Harlech and Beaumaris have conspicuously strong gatehouse towers. Beaumaris especially, the last of the series and never finished, fulfils the classic ideal of the castle, with a square inner bailey enclosed by massive walls with round corner towers, two symmetrical gatehouse-keeps and an outer wall lapped by an encircling moat. Much credit is due to the mason in charge, Master James of St George.

There is nothing in England which compares with these new single-minded castles. The nearest equivalent is probably Goodrich in Herefordshire, where Aymer de Valence, who had much experience in foreign wars, modernised an old castle in the 1280s by enclosing the old keep in a high-walled rectangle with

Tintagel is always linked with the name of King Arthur and said to be his birthplace, but the association was first made only in the 1140s when Geoffrey of Monmouth brought out his History of the Britons. There is nothing to explain why he made the connection, although recent archaeological finds indicate that Tintagel was a place of great wealth in the Dark Ages. By coincidence, the castle was also begun in the 1140s for the Earl of Cornwall. At this time Tintagel was a peninsula and the castle was laid out along its narrow neck. Over the years the sea washed the neck away and the remains of the inner parts of the castle are now marooned on an island, leaving the outer parts on the cliffs ashore.

round corner towers. Projecting spurs were added to the feet of these towers, and a high priority was put on strengthening the gatehouse by building a substantial barbican. Similar attention was paid to improving the gatehouses of many other English castles at about this time; two surviving examples are Rockingham Castle in Northamptonshire and Tonbridge Castle in Kent. But there were also those who valued their domestic comfort as much as their defences. At Carisbrooke in the Isle of Wight Isabella Forz improved the castle between 1270 and 1290 by building a new chapel, great chamber and other rooms. At Restormel in Cornwall during the same period Edmund of Almaine lined the circular wall of the old shell-keep with a luxurious and sophisticated apartment, to make himself a residence which had more than a little in common with Frederick II's octagonal Castel del Monte in Apulia.

By the beginning of the fourteenth century the war with the Welsh was finished and there was no campaigning on English soil for a long period. But the early decades were a time of considerable discontent at the lower levels of society which produced a lawless climate. There was a marked increase in the number of noblemen who applied to the crown for a licence to crenellate their walls against peasant bandits and in the number of moats dug by yeomen farmers to protect their houses and livestock. This uncomfortable social climate continued well into the second half of the century, which was further overshadowed by the Black Death. The Hundred Years War provoked by the English claim to the throne of France, and continuing disputes with the Scots, shifted the military focus to the northern border and the southern coastal counties. Right at the beginning of the century the walls of the little castle at Aydon in Northumberland were crenellated. In the same county but further up the social scale the Percy family re-fortified their castles at Alnwick and Warkworth, while their Neville rivals re-fortified Raby in Durham. Further south, Edward III splendidly rebuilt Windsor Castle as a home for the Order of the Garter, founded in 1348, and also built two forts to defend the Thames estuary at Hadleigh in Essex and Queenborough in Kent. In the 1380s Kentish castles like Cooling, Scotney and Saltwood were equipped with machicolated walls and imposing gatehouses, while across the border in Sussex Sir Edward Dalyngrydge obtained a royal licence to crenellate – which in this case meant to build a brand-new castle – at Bodiam on the River Rother.

Restormel is one of the best pieces of military architecture in Cornwall, probably built to command a crossing-point on the River Fowey. A ringwork consisting of an earth bank and a tall motte topped by a timber castle with a stone gateway were built here in about 1100. The present outer wall dates from about 1200. The final additions were made by Edward, Earl of Cornwall, who built a continuous ring of living rooms inside the great wall in about 1280. They seem to have been luxurious and sophisticated apartments, almost as if Edward was attempting to turn this circular castle into a villa.

A djoining the Bishop of Winchester's Palace on the north side are the ruins of Old Wolvesey Castle. During the Middle Ages Winchester was the richest English see and its bishops were influential men. One of the most powerful was Henry of Blois, grandson of William the Conqueror. Soon after his appointment in 1129 he enlarged the existing palace by adding a new great hall. Henry was deeply involved in the machinations of the civil war between Stephen and Matilda for the English throne and during the 1140s and 1150s he prudently strengthened his palace by adding new perimeter walls and a strong tower or keep, which can be seen in the foreground of this view. Behind them in shadow are the foundation outlines of the great hall.

Although new, Bodiam was in some ways old-fashioned. Its moated rectangular plan, with drum towers at the four corners, recalled the castles built in North Wales a century before. On the other hand, the walls were furnished with gun-loops and the ample living rooms ranged round the inside wall showed signs of improvement. A similar tendency to comfort can be seen in some northern castles, like Bolton in Swaledale, Yorkshire. Begun in 1379, Bolton Castle offered twelve individual lodgings and eight household suites round the four sides of a tall rectangular tower. Equally significant for the future was the castle built by Sir John de la Mare at Nunney in Somerset. Sir John had served with the army in France and he built a compact moated tower-house, closely resembling a type which was becoming popular in that country.

At Nunney the living rooms are badly lit and packed rather tightly, making it difficult to imagine that the castle was ever very comfortable. The same cannot be said of Wardour Castle in Wiltshire, built by Lord Lovel after 1393. Here the main building was basically hexagonal in plan, with a hexagonal court-yard in the centre for light and air and a great hall on the first floor with tall and elegant windows. Wardour was primarily a strong but convenient house for a wealthy nobleman. Another example of similar type was the new keep at Warkworth in Northumberland, built for the Percys at the very end of the century. They were a warlike family and Warkworth keep is more formidable than Wardour, but there is the same striving for architectural effect, partly through symmetry, and the same care in the planning of the elaborate private apartment. More elaborate still were the new living quarters at Kenilworth in Warwickshire. Between 1391 and 1393 John of Gaunt employed the master mason Robert Skyllington on a rebuilding which produced the most splendid great hall of the fourteenth century.

The show of wealth in these later fourteenth-century castles was only possible for those noble families who were able to supplement their falling incomes from the land by other means, usually a series of arranged marriages. One effect of these liaisons was to concentrate several major castles in the hands of a single private owner, who seldom had the inclination to build more. There were similar problems in the fifteenth century and most new castles were built by social upstarts and the newly rich. In the 1440s there was a wave of building activity by veterans of the French wars: Sir John Fastolf's Caister in Norfolk

(1433–1448), Ralph Cromwell's Tattershall in Lincolnshire (1430–1450) and Sir Roger Fiennes's Herstmonceaux in Sussex (1440). All three were built in brick, then a new, expensive and ostentatious material. They had the appearance of castles, with prominent towers, and their defences were perfectly sufficient to deter robbers or jealous neighbours, but they were not exclusively military. The walls were pierced by large windows to light the large rooms inside. Kirby Muxloe Castle, built in the 1480s by Lord Hastings, was another such. The brick walls here were prettily decorated with the Hastings badge, but they were also pierced by round openings intended for guns.

The arrival of efficient artillery put an end to the traditional castle, or rather turned the ideas of military engineers towards new kinds of fortification. In 1494 the French troops of Charles VIII marched through northern Italy with their siege guns, reducing fortress after fortress with astonishing rapidity. From the first years of the sixteenth century in England there was a gradual disseverance of forts and houses. The Tudor monarchs and their nobles still set considerable value on the possession of traditional castles, but this was more a recognition of their symbolic power than of their strategic value. Indeed, the building of castle-style houses, and houses with gate-towers, continued well into the sixteenth century. Cardinal Wolsey's Hampton Court is one example, Titchfield Abbey in Hampshire is another, though neither can compare with the extraordinary Layer Marney in Essex, built in the early 1520s. Even a century later, the castle style still retained a place in English architecture, though by this time it was as a romantic symbol of an Arthurian Golden Age. To see this one need only go to Bolsover in Derbyshire, where the mediaeval castle was re-constructed by Charles Cavendish as a romantic folly in the reign of James I.

The new generation of military forts reversed the emphasis of late-mediaeval castle building in such a way as to deprive the type of its more obvious attractions, at least for the private owner. Tall towers and proud walls were now a thing of the past; artillery platforms needed to be massively strong, with walls as thick as those of a mediaeval keep, and also very compact and low-lying to avoid presenting a good target. During the course of the sixteenth century the techniques of military engineering developed rapidly, especially on the European mainland. On this side of the Channel, Henry VIII maintained a close personal interest in the new warfare. Following his break with the Papacy in the

The red stone ruins of Brougham stand in a peaceful spot by the side of the River Lowther. This river crossing has always been important, a point witnessed by the remains of a Roman army camp nearby. The tall keep was built in about 1170 and immediately next to it are the inner and outer gateways, a slightly unusual arrangement which gave Brougham a formidably strong entrance. Across the inner court are the living rooms including the great hall, which are now very ruinous. Brougham fell into decay in the later Middle Ages, but was thoroughly restored in the 1650s by Lady Anne Clifford, a woman of formidable character who restored all her four northern castles and lived in them in great style.

All that remains of Orford Castle is the tall keep overlooking the Suffolk marshes and the sea. Nevertheless, the keep is impressive and also historically important because it was one of the first in England to abandon the traditional square or oblong shape in favour of something more elaborate – in this case an eighteen-sided cylinder with three square turrets. Orford was a royal castle, built between 1165 and 1172. King Henry II took a particular interest in fortification. We know from contemporary documents that he employed Alnoth, keeper of the king's houses, to supervise the building work, which cost in all £1413.9s.2d, a huge sum for the time. Orford was finished just in time to uphold the king's authority in a serious rebellion.

From the importance of the harbour below and the natural strength of the site, Dover Castle has been called the Key of England. In Roman times there were two lighthouses, of which one survives next to the church. Dominating the castle is Henry II's great rectangular keep built in the 1180s, which is the strongest, finest and most elaborate example built in the twelfth century. Henry also built the inner curtain wall and part of the outer, with the projecting wall towers influenced perhaps by crusader castles. In the siege of 1216 the main gate of the outer wall (in the foreground here) proved a weak point and was later blocked up and replaced by a new gate entered through the much stronger Constable's Tower. The last army detachments left Dover only in 1958.

1530s and faced with the threat of invasion, he equipped the shores facing the Continent with the last word in modern defences. Fortifications were constructed along the south and east coasts from Milford Haven to Hull, to counter any attempted landings, and new castles, or rather block-houses, were erected at strategic points. Five were built along the Thames, three at Dover, but the biggest and most important of the series were the 'Three Castles Which Keep the Downs', in other words Deal, Walmer and Sandown, which protected the best safe roadstead for ships on the coast of Kent. Little of Sandown remains, but the other two survive intact. Both have a squat circular central tower – still known as the keep – closely surrounded by an outer wall made up of semi-circular bastions which carried the guns. From the air the forts look purely geometrical, the four bastions at Walmer making a quatrefoil, the six at Deal a hexfoil. In the event, an invasion never materialised, and although several of the forts saw action in the Civil War, their compact design had long been superseded by the bastion system

A closer view of Henry II's great keep at Dover, which also shows the buildings clustered along the inner face of the surrounding wall. There are few other castles in England where such buildings, which were universal in mediaeval castles, still survive in use.

Beeston Castle stands on an isolated crag of red sandstone, commanding a view which stretches from Derbyshire to Wales. The builder was Rannulf de Blundeville, 7th Earl of Chester, who put the works in hand in the 1220s. Many of the defensive arrangements were clearly influenced by the military practice of the crusades, in particular the choice of a site where natural cliffs rather than walls formed the main protection. The inner ward of the castle has cliffs on three sides and the strong front wall stood behind a ditch cut deep into the natural rock. This wall was improved at the end of the century by King Edward I and the round-towered gatehouse bears more than a passing resemblance to Edward's castles in north Wales.

Goodrich Castle in Hereford stands on a low outcrop of red sandstone overlooking the River Wye. Nearly square, with a great round tower at each corner of the curtain wall, it is the cousin of Welsh castles like Harlech and Beaumaris. The tall rectangular keep of white stone is the oldest part of the castle and dates from the middle of the twelfth century; the walls and towers surrounding it were built in the 1280s. Goodrich is approached through a well-preserved barbican which defended the entrance. A vaulted gatehouse leads to the central court, with the ruins of the main living rooms, including the hall, the chapel and the garderobe block with its privies emptying into the dry moat.

Carisbrooke was the strongest castle on the Isle of Wight. Traces of a probable Roman fort can still be seen in the form of stone walls. The Normans built a tall motte on top of the Roman walls and a bailey enclosing the living quarters. By 1136 the original wooden palisade on the motte had been replaced in stone, and the curtain wall round the bailey had also been rebuilt. The living accommodation here was made more comfortable in the second half of the thirteenth century by Isabella Fortibus, widow of the Earl of Albermarle. After her death the castle came to the crown and a new gatehouse (on the left in this view) was added in the 1330s. Some further improvements were made to the accommodation in the fifteenth century but they are of less importance than the work on the defences a century later. Between 1597 and 1600 the corners of the old wall were strengthened and the whole castle was enclosed in new defences of the most modern type, designed to cope with artillery. They were built under the supervision of Federigo Gianibelli, a famous Italian engineer.

Nunney Castle lies among the houses of the village at the bottom of a valley – a bad site for a castle but a very attractive one. Nunney is really a tall fortified house with a pair of fat round towers at either end. The building is surrounded by a moat and the moat itself was once enclosed by a wall on three sides. This castle was built in 1373 by Sir John de la Mare, who had made his fortune from the wars in France, and it must have looked very French when the main block still had its steep pitched roof and the four towers their conical caps. The rooms were arranged on four floors, with the kitchens at ground level, the servants on the first floor, the great hall on the second floor and two more large rooms on the third. Nunney was beseiged in the Civil War and the north side was weakened by gunfire. Shortly afterwards all the floors were removed and over two hundred years later, on Christmas Day 1910, the north wall (on the far side in this view) collapsed.

Aydon Castle is a rather modest affair, with a walled outer bailey and an inner bailey mostly taken up by a cluster of domestic buildings which are perched on the edge of a wooded slope falling to the Cor Burn. The walls were probably finished in about 1305, which makes Aydon a very early example of something intended to be a fortified house rather than a castle proper.

The outer ward and grounds of Old Wardour Castle were landscaped in the middle of the eighteenth century to enhance the prospect from a great new Palladian house nearby. This has given Wardour the flavour of a romantic ruin enhanced by the pretty Gothick banqueting house overlooking the lake. But the castle is basically the building begun by Lord Lovel in about 1393 – a tower house built for lavish entertainment and domestic comfort. Later alterations for Sir Matthew Arundell in the 1570s improved the comforts further and many of the windows were enlarged. The castle was besieged twice in the English Civil War and the south side was destroyed.`

Warkworth is in many ways the most interesting of all the Northumbrian castles. It has a handsome site by the River Coquet and rears up above the small town huddled inland from the cold North Sea. From the twelfth century onwards Warkworth was an important military base and the basic layout of the castle was established at that time. The walls and gatehouse date from before 1215 but in 1332 the castle passed into the hands of the Percy family, earls of Northumberland, and Warkworth became their favourite residence. They carried out many alterations and improvements, of which the most notable was the rebuilding of the old keep in the early fifteenth century as a symmetrical tower-house.

*D*eal was one of the
'Three Great
Castles Which Keep the
Downs', built in the late
1530s as part of Henry
VIII's improvement of
coastal defences; the
others were Walmer and
Sandgate. The flat strip
of coast on which they
were built overlooked a
stretch of sea which was
protected from the worst
of the Channel weather
by the Goodwin Sands
and had become an
important anchorage for
sailing ships. Thanks to
some rebuilding after
bomb-damage in the last
war Deal has regained
much of its original
character – a thoroughly
utilitarian gun-platform
with a beautiful
geometrical plan.

The spectacular ½-mile-wide great lake which defended the south and west sides of the castle has been dry for three hundred years, but Kenilworth is still one of the grandest castles in England. The outer circle of walls mostly dates from about 1205 but the impressive group of deep pink sandstone buildings at the centre of the castle is of three different periods. The massive keep with its square corner towers was built in about 1180 and is the oldest part, although the windows were modernised in the sixteenth century. Curving round from the keep (on the left in this view) is a suite of rooms erected for John of Gaunt in the last years of the fourteenth century. In 1563 Kenilworth passed to Robert Dudley, Earl of Leicester and favourite of Queen Elizabeth. He treated the castle like a great Elizabethan house and built a block of grand apartments for distinguished visitors. Queen Elizabeth paid several visits to Kenilworth and Sir Walter Scott's novel of that name paints a vivid picture of her visit in 1575, when she stayed for nineteen days of continuous entertainment.

John of Gaunt's buildings at Kenilworth. At the centre of the group is the ruined great hall with magnificent traceried windows and moulded panels rising the full height of the building. In its heyday this was one of the finest rooms in mediaeval England.

Kirby Muxloe Castle had a sad and short life. It was begun in 1480 for William, Lord Hastings, a rich nobleman and a supporter of the Yorkist King Edward IV. Three years later he was suddenly executed by Richard III for suspected treason and his new castle was never finished. It was intended to be a typical late fifteenth-century castle, as much mansion as fortress, with a rectangular curtain wall defended by towers at regular intervals and surrounded by a moat. The main living rooms were built against the inner side of the walls. One novelty was the use of red brick patterning. Another innovation was the provision of keyhole-shaped openings for guns. The accounts for the building work have survived and it is possible to chart every step of the process. The masons were John Cowper and Robert Staynforth (who had worked on the earlier brick castle at Tattershall in Lincolnshire) and a Dutchman called Anthony Yzebrand was employed to supervise the making of the bricks.

of defence, best exemplified in the walls of Berwick upon Tweed, built in the 1560s. A southern example of the same system can be seen at Carisbrooke in the Isle of Wight, where the old castle was strengthened in the 1590s by a series of great bastions designed by the Italian engineer Federigo Gianibelli. The intention of these massive arrowheads of solid earth faced with stone was partly to distance hostile artillery from the walls but mainly to surround the old castle with a flat and featureless area which could be easily swept with gunfire. The bastion system continued to develop during the seventeenth century at the hands of exponents like Vauban in France and reached its maximum sophistication in the late seventeenth and early eighteenth centuries.

From the 1530s onwards most fort-building in England was concentrated along the coasts. From the Napoleonic Wars there remain the Martello Towers and from the 1860s the various great fortifications built by Lord Palmerston's government. From the intervening period, the fort at Tilbury on the Thames is in many ways the finest surviving example of late seventeenth-century military engineering in England. Its only rival is the Royal Citadel at Plymouth. Tilbury was originally the site of one of Henry VIII's shore forts, placed on the north bank of the Thames at a point immediately opposite the town of Gravesend where the river narrows sufficiently for heavy guns to command its full width. In

Tilbury Fort is the best preserved and in many ways the finest surviving example of late seventeenth-century military engineering in England. The fort was designed by Sir Bernard de Gomme, chief engineer and surveyor of the ordnance to Charles II, in response to the highly successful Dutch raid up the Thames and Medway in 1667. Work began in 1670 on the site of an earlier fort of the 1530s and was more or less completed by 1683. Tilbury was intended to command the full width of the River Thames, in conjunction with Gravesend on the opposite bank. It was designed at a time when artillery was the dominant weapon, so the walls were mostly thick low-lying banks of earth to withstand the shock of bombardment. The heaviest guns were mounted on the river side, while on the land side the fort was defended by complicated geometrical outworks with a double line of moats.

From the early years of the eighteenth century Walmer Castle was the official residence of the lords warden of the Cinque Ports. Some of them, like William Pitt, Lord Liverpool and especially the Duke of Wellington used the castle as their home. The original austere accommodation was hardly suitable for an official residence and the first resident warden, the Duke of Dorset, extended the old keep with a suite of living rooms. Many of the windows have been enlarged over the years and now the fort, with its charming semi-formal garden, has a very unthreatening appearance.

Walmer Castle originally had a simpler plan than its contemporary sister fort at Deal. It was built as a quatrefoil with a circular tower or keep in the middle, but this simplicity was muddled as the castle was altered during the course of its life as the official residence of the lord warden of the Cinque Ports.

the years after the Civil War Charles II began a reorganisation of the country's defences and had already considered strengthening Tilbury, when the question was suddenly made acute by a highly successful Dutch raid up the Thames and Medway in 1667. Charles's chief engineer, Sir Bernard de Gomme, submitted fresh plans for improving the defences and in the ten years after 1670 Tilbury was transformed into a powerful gun-battery commanding the river, with elaborate outworks on the landward side. These outworks were based on the shape of a pentagon, and included two moats in addition to the ramparts. Perhaps because of its strength, Tilbury was never used for its intended purpose and its only military success was as an anti-aircraft battery in the First World War.

While single-minded constructions like Tilbury can rarely be turned to other than military uses, mediaeval castles have proved more adaptable. This process of adaption started early; the same Robert Smythson who was responsible for the romantic Jacobean castle at Bolsover also modernised the keep at Wardour by inserting larger windows. Such later alterations have often confused the mediaeval remains. At the other end of the scale are those castles which now consist only of an encircling wall. In both cases it requires a necessary effort to visualise the original hybrid state of these buildings which were both fortifications and houses.

HOUSES
AND PALACES

❊

mong the many properties in the care of English Heritage, far outnumbered by Roman remains and the ruins of abbeys and castles, is a small group of what were once private houses. Perhaps mansions would be a better name, since most of them were built for wealthy and aristocratic patrons. They have come into the hands of English Heritage – and its predecessors – in different ways and for various reasons. Osborne House in the Isle of Wight was once a royal palace, Audley End, Belsay, Bolsover, The Grange and Kirby Hall were either ruinous or friendless, while Marble Hill, Kenwood and Ranger's House at Blackheath were adopted on the demise of the Greater London Council. They make a diverse collection but, by coincidence, these houses illustrate some of the more important developments in English domestic architecture from the time of Queen Elizabeth I to the time of Queen Victoria.

For several centuries before Elizabeth the principal feature of the English mediaeval house was the hall, in northern England called the housebody, which served as the living room and dining room of the whole household. Whatever their size, halls followed the same general arrangement with an entrance at one end leading into a passage (known as a 'screens passage') across the bottom of the hall with a high table at the other end. In earlier years an open fire in the centre of the room provided the heat, in later years a chimney was provided on one of the side walls. Beyond the screens passage were the kitchen and serving rooms and behind the high table the private rooms of the lord and his family. The earliest halls sometimes served as a common dormitory as well, but from the thirteenth

The palace at Bishop's Waltham in Hampshire was begun in about 1135 by Henry of Blois, Bishop of Winchester, and rebuilt and extended several times afterwards. It remained in use until the seventeenth century but was ruined in the Civil War and abandoned afterwards. The palace was contained in a rectangular site enclosed by a water-filled moat, of which parts still survive. The main buildings were in two ranges, of which the west range contained the great hall and also the kitchen, which is shown in the foreground of this view.

century there was a proliferation of other chambers to serve as private dining rooms and withdrawing rooms. These arrangements prevailed in palaces, in castles, in the later semi-fortified or unfortified manor houses of the English countryside and in the much more modest houses of farmers and townsmen. In the cramped space available in castles the rooms were often compactly planned out of necessity but elsewhere they were often allowed to straggle as a series of separate buildings. In the houses of the wealthy there was a need to provide for a large household of retainers and it gradually became common practice to dispose all the living rooms round a central courtyard. When the house was also the centre of a country estate there were often farm buildings nearby.

Minster Lovell Hall in Oxfordshire, ravishingly sited in a bend of the River Windrush, is a good example of a late-mediaeval nobleman's house. The name reveals the origin of the place, which was founded as a minster or monastery in the ninth century, and later became a dependent priory of the abbey of Ivry in France. The religious foundation was suppressed in 1414 along with many other small alien priories, but the title to the manor and much of the land were retained by the Lovell family. In about 1430 the old manor house on the site was rebuilt by William, 7th Baron Lovell, an extremely wealthy man. His new house was built close to the priory church round three sides of a courtyard which opened towards the river. The centre of the main range was taken up by the great hall, the solar or private room and the chapel – these being the three most important rooms in any late-mediaeval house. The west end of the main range and the west wing contained a series of good-sized rooms with fireplaces, which were probably for other members of the family or household. The east wing was given over to the kitchen, bake-house, pantry and a stable. Behind this wing at a respectable distance from the house were the buildings of the manorial farm, including the dovecot which was a valuable source of fresh meat during the winter months. Some time later in the fifteenth century the open end of the courtyard was closed with a wall and a tower was added to the west wing. The reason for this alteration is not known, but presumably it was intended to make the house a little more secure, if not from a serious attack, then at least from the attentions of casual robbers.

A century later England was a more orderly country, and many Elizabethan noblemen provided themselves with larger and more modern houses. The great

Clustered round the main house at Minster Lovell are the church of St Kenelm, also rebuilt by Lord Lovell, and the barns and other utilitarian structures belonging to the home farm, of which the most conspicuous is the dovecot, which provided a ready supply of fresh meat in the winter.

The ruins at Minster Lovell are those of a manor house rebuilt in the first half of the fifteenth century by William, Lord Lovell. They stand on the banks of the little River Windrush in a setting which is romantically beautiful. The rooms were arranged round three sides of a courtyard, with the great hall, solar and chapel in the centre. The south side of the court was originally open to the river.

Cardinal Wolsey's enormous red-brick manor house of Hampton Court (see previous page) was built on the bank of the River Thames between 1514 and 1520. The house originally had two courtyards: a large outer court and a small inner court around which the main rooms were grouped. King Henry VIII took the house for himself, enlarged and enriched it and turned it into a palace. When William and Mary came to the throne in 1688 they determined to rival Louis XIV at Versailles and commanded Sir Christopher Wren to rebuild the whole palace on a larger scale and in the Classical style. The work was left half-finished after Queen Mary's death in 1698 but Wolsey's buildings and Wren's co-exist quite happily. The formal gardens around the palace belong to the early years of the eighteenth century; they have survived well, although many casualties of the great hurricane of October 1987 can be seen lying across the banks of the great canal.

The gateway and principal entrance leading to the base court of Cardinal Wolsey's great house. The front is decorated in a rather traditional fashion with battlements and patterned brickwork, but signs of the coming Renaissance are the terracotta roundels set into the gate-towers; they are by the Italian Giovanni da Majano.

hall was still their central reception room, supplemented in most cases by an even more splendid great chamber, but the number of other living rooms was greatly increased and these mansions were usually two or three storeys high. The queen herself encouraged her more prominent courtiers like Robert Cecil and Christopher Hatton in the building of enormously expensive mansions. Although there are similarities of planning between them, such houses borrowed their ornament from a variety of sources in Italy, France and the Low Countries of Belgium and Holland. Illustrated books of architecture and design played a crucial part in this exchange. With their help both noble patrons and stonemasons could improve on the traditional ways of building.

Kirby Hall in Northamptonshire illustrates many of these aspects of Elizabethan house-building. The foundation stone of Sir Humphrey Stafford's new house was laid in 1570 by John Thorpe, then five years old. His father Thomas Thorpe was a master mason and presumably in charge of the building. The main house was built round a courtyard; on the south side were the great hall, the great chamber, the parlour and the kitchen; the east range contained lodgings or apartments; the west range had lodgings on the ground floor and a long gallery above. The main entrance was through the north range, whose ground floor on the courtyard side was an open *loggia* with an arcaded front. This was a feature which derived ultimately from the Italian Renaissance and can be found in several Elizabethan houses, including Hatfield. The particular arrangement at Kirby, with the *loggia* on the courtyard side of the entrance range, has affinities with French houses of the time, like Anet in Normandy. Another French feature, almost unprecedented in England at the time, was the use of giant pilasters to decorate the courtyard walls. The idea was probably taken from a book, and other books supplied ornamental details. Two central pilasters on the north range have capitals copied from *L'Architettura* by the Italian Sebastiano Serlio, and arabesque decoration on their lower parts from John Shute's *First and Chief Grounds of Architecture* published in 1563.

Humphrey Stafford died in 1575 and Kirby, still unfinished, was bought by the queen's favourite, Christopher Hatton, who eventually became lord chancellor of England. Between 1575 and his death in 1591 Hatton completed the building work and improved the accommodation by adding a new main stair and more rooms in a southwest wing near the hall. His new additions have elaborate roof-gables with the strapwork decoration called Flemish, which was becoming fashionable in the last years of the sixteenth century. Although the fortunes of the Hatton family fluctuated during the new century, the house was twice more improved. In the late 1630s Christopher III gave the house a new front and made other modifications in a version of the Italian Classical style which Inigo Jones had introduced at court. The mason for the work and perhaps the architect was Nicholas Stone; as master mason to the king he knew Jones's works at first-hand. Half a century later in the 1680s, Christopher IV, who was a noted horticulturalist, improved the existing formal garden layout to make what his brother called 'ye finest garden in England'. Part of his layout was restored in the 1930s and modern excavation may reveal more about the layout.

The same Flemish style which Christopher Hatton had used at Kirby informed the building of Audley End, begun in about 1605 for Thomas Howard, Earl of Suffolk. The building was designed by the Dutch sculptor Bernhard Johnson or Janssen and is important in the development of English architecture as one of the first great houses in the Anglo-Flemish style. Howard, who became Lord Treasurer to James I in 1614, spent a huge sum of money on his new house. There was originally a great outer courtyard with elaborate decoration, but this was pulled down in 1721 to make the house of manageable size. In 1752 the eastern range of the inner court was also pulled down. The stonework of the outer walls has been so patched and re-faced that there is virtually nothing left visible of the earl's original mansion except the two elaborate porches with their fantastic decoration.

One aspect of the Elizabethan mind which seems foreign to us is the passion for conceits, in the sense of ingenious, witty or fanciful notions. Perhaps the most compelling example of such a conceit in architectural terms is Sir Thomas Tresham's triangular lodge at Rushton in Northamptonshire. Tresham was a local notable and, more significantly, a Roman Catholic convert, who spent most of his subsequent life in prison for his faith. In the mid-1590s during a brief respite he improved the family house at Rushton and built in the park there a small lodge house. The walls are vividly striped with ironstone and everything about the building is based on the number three. The plan is a triangle, each wall is 33 feet 4 inches long (one-third of 100 feet) and has three storeys, each storey has three windows and so on. In addition, the walls are inscribed with various

Kirby Hall, Northamptonshire is an Elizabethan mansion built for Sir Humphrey Stafford in the five years after 1570. All the main rooms were ranged round a large courtyard decorated with Classical motifs copied from fashionable foreign pattern-books. Entrance was through the north range, which has an open loggia on the courtyard side – another borrowing from abroad. The south wing with its two bow windows contains additional reception rooms and was added after Sir Humphrey's time by the queen's favourite Sir Christopher Hatton, who eventually became lord chancellor of England.

*T*he formal gardens at Kirby are a re-creation of the arrangement of the 1680s, when Christopher Hatton III, who was a noted horticulturalist, laid out what his brother described as 'ye finest garden in England'.

*A*udley End was originally one of the largest Jacobean mansions in the country, built round two courtyards. In the eighteenth century the huge outer court was completely demolished and one side of the inner court was also removed to make the house a more convenient size. The gardens were landscaped by Capability Brown in the 1760s and they contain a number of elegant garden buildings designed by Robert Adam. Among them is the circular Ring Hill Temple, seen here in the far distance beyond the river.

Thomas Tresham's triangular lodge at Rushton, Northamptonshire, built to symbolise the Holy Trinity. It was begun in 1594 and completed in 1597.

dates, numbers and texts, including part of the preface to the Catholic Mass. Tresham's lodge is an allegory of the Holy Trinity and also a pun on his family name and the trefoil or three-leaved plant which was the family badge.

Something of the same spirit can be perceived in the buildings of Bolsover Castle in Derbyshire. The site is an old one, since the commanding position atop a ridge had been chosen in the Middle Ages as an excellent location for a castle, but when Charles Cavendish acquired the lease in 1608 he set about planning a replacement for the ruined castle buildings. His mother, the formidable Bess of Hardwick, was an enthusiast for building and Charles inherited both her enthusiasm and the services of Robert Smythson, her favourite designer. Smythson was an original and inventive architect and at Bolsover he planned to replace the old castle with a modern version of the same thing, exploiting the dramatic site for poetic effect. On the highest part of the site he placed the Little Keep, a compact house containing the private family apartments decked out with battlements and a tower in pseudo-mediaeval style. It is a theatrical conception and may well have provided the backdrop when Ben Jonson's masque *Love's Welcome to Bolsover* was performed here before Charles I in 1634. Stretching away from the keep, but linked to it by a bridge, is the Terrace Range containing the great hall, long gallery and the other more splendid and public rooms. Robert Smythson died in 1614 shortly after the foundations were laid and Sir Charles died three years later. The unfinished house passed to Sir William Cavendish who retained Robert's son John Smythson to continue the building. He fitted out the rooms of the Little Keep with their lavish painted decoration and completed the Terrace Range in a mixed style which combined elaborate Jacobean gables, late Gothic mouldings over the windows and elements of the new Classical style of Inigo Jones, reinterpreted without reference to the accepted laws of proportion. In the 1620s and 1630s Sir William enlarged the Terrace Range with a suite of state rooms and built a new range containing a handsome riding school with a forge and all the necessary appurtenances, to gratify his interest in *haute ecole*. Taken together, these buildings are among the most interesting of their date in England. There could hardly be a better illustration of the diverse influences which affected architecture during the decades before the Civil War.

More modest in scale, though displaying many of the same architectural features, is the Dutch House, otherwise known as Kew Palace, which stands by the Thames in one corner of the Royal Botanical Gardens and is administered by the Historic Royal Palaces Agency. Built in 1631, this was originally the house of a city merchant of Dutch descent named Samuel Fortrey, and it is one of a group of similar houses of this decade which survive in or near the capital. All of them are built of red brick and were probably put up by master craftsmen belonging to the London city livery companies. Their architecture shows the Bolsover mixture of tall Dutch gables and the Classical orders, but the decoration is cut in elaborate brickwork, which by now was cheaper than stone. Most of these houses, including the Dutch House, are compactly planned as a single block with living rooms, kitchen and servants' quarters under one roof and not spread out in the traditional patrician way. By a series of accidents, this modest merchant's house was pressed into service in 1802 as a temporary residence for King George III and his family, while their new Gothic palace was being built nearby. In the event, the palace was never completed and the Dutch House continued to serve as a royal retreat until Queen Charlotte died here in 1818.

Bolsover Castle stands on a ridge of land overlooking a landscape of farmland and coal mines. There was a mediaeval castle here, but it was mostly destroyed to make way for the romantic fantasy house of Sir Charles Cavendish and his son Sir William who became Earl of Newcastle. The oldest part is the Little Keep intended for family use, designed by Robert Smythson and begun in about 1610; stretching away from it is the long roofless range which contained the state apartments, while beyond is the great riding school. Sir William Cavendish published an important work on dressage in 1658 and it is pleasant to record that his riding school is still in use.

The Little Keep at Bolsover has a ceremonial forecourt, which is of no practical use except to make the main approach more impressive. Annexed to the keep is the Fountain Garden, a private space set aside from the great outer court, whose walls are built on the foundations of the wall enclosing the inner bailey of the mediaeval castle.

In 1631 a City merchant called Samuel Fortrey built himself a small country house by the river at Kew. It was a tall Dutch-looking building with a great deal of brick ornament and shaped gables. By the end of the eighteenth century the house had become part of the royal estate at Kew. George III and Queen Charlotte moved in as a temporary measure in 1801 and the queen stayed there till 1818. In the nineteenth century the Kew estate became the Royal Botanical Gardens and the Dutch House was included in its boundaries. Since the last war the land behind the house has been laid out in formal seventeenth-century fashion, complete with a mount at the far end from which to view both the flower beds and the river.

The garden behind the Dutch House has recently been laid out in a modern version of a typical seventeenth-century arrangement, compact in size and wholly formal, with rectangular beds and *parterres*, tightly clipped hedges and, at the bottom of the garden, a small grassy mound with a gazebo from which the whole can be viewed. Another example of the same sort of thing can be seen at Boscobel House in Shropshire. The house itself is a very modest timber-framed building which probably dates from about 1630, but it has a claim to fame as the place where King Charles II hid after losing the Civil War Battle of Worcester in 1651. After the Restoration Boscobel was celebrated for its part in saving the king and illustrations of that time show the formal garden and also the motte with its arbour in which Charles spent a whole day resting. In the seventeenth century Boscobel lay in a wood and at one point Charles was forced to hide in the branches of an oak tree. A short distance from the house, in the middle of a field, is preserved a large tree which is supposed to be a child of the 'royal oak'. The original was carried away piecemeal by early souvenir-hunters.

The characteristic architecture of the four decades from the Restoration to Queen Anne is the robust English version of the continental Baroque style as used by architects like Sir Christopher Wren and his colleagues in the royal Office of Works. Although fully conversant with the rules of proportion which should govern the use of the Classical orders, these architects handled Classical forms with considerable freedom and often with striking effect. Sir John Vanbrugh's Blenheim Palace is probably the most dramatic example of the English Baroque, but there are many other examples including the ruined Appuldurcombe in the Isle of Wight, which is in the care of English Heritage. In the second decade of the eighteenth century a new taste developed for a more 'correct' form of architecture which was claimed to be based more closely on the example of the ancients, of Andrea Palladio's north Italian villas and of Inigo Jones's works in England. One of its leading propagandists was the Scottish architect Colen Campbell. In 1715 Campbell brought out the first of the three volumes of his *Vitruvius Britannicus*, which contained illustrations of English buildings inspired by Roman models.

A few years later Richard Boyle, 3rd Earl of Burlington, a nobleman with a keen personal interest in art and architecture, visited Italy and spent some months studying Palladio's buildings at first hand. Shortly after his return in

*B*oscobel is a small timber-framed house of the 1630s where the young King Charles II hid after his defeat at the Battle of Worcester in 1651. In later years the house was enlarged and became a farmhouse, but the older part still looks much as it does in the popular views of the Restoration period. Most of these views also show the garden, laid out in the formal and functional seventeenth-century manner with rectangular beds and hedges, a mount and an orchard. In the early 19th century this layout was restored – a remarkable antiquarian exercise of the Romantic period.

company with a painter named William Kent he determined to build what might be described as a temple to the new style in the grounds of his old family house at Chiswick. In 1723 he designed for himself a villa based loosely on Palladio's Villa Capra outside Vicenza in northern Italy. The Chiswick villa followed Italian precedents in many respects. The front was marked by a handsome Classical portico approached by a double staircase, all the principal rooms were on the first floor as in Italian *palazzi* and both the tri-partite windows of the principal floor and the raised dome were derived from buildings in Italy. The intended function of the building is not clear. The suite of richly decorated and exquisitely proportioned rooms on the first floor may have been meant for the display of sculpture, paintings and other objects of value. On the other hand, the rooms could have served as replacements for the old-fashioned living rooms in the adjoining mansion.

Much of the decoration inside the villa was the work of William Kent, who went on to be one of the more influential designers of the Palladian movement

A short distance from Boscobel House in the middle of a field is a large oak tree, growing on the site of the former 'royal oak' in which the king hid for a day of his time at Boscobel. The original tree, which stood in the middle of a wood, was carried away piecemeal by souvenir hunters but the present tree is said to have sprung from one of its acorns.

Chiswick House was designed by Richard Boyle, 3rd Earl of Burlington, and built c. 1725–1729 as an extension to an old Jacobean mansion belonging to his family. Burlington was a great admirer of the north Italian villas and farmhouses designed by Andrea Palladio in the sixteenth century and his new building was based loosely on Palladio's Villa Capra near Vicenza. The triple windows were derived from Roman baths, the raised dome came from other Italian villas and all the principal rooms were on the first floor in the manner of Italian palazzi. The Jacobean mansion has long been demolished, leaving the villa, together with the summer parlour and the link building which formed the original means of communication between it and the Jacobean house.

during the first half of the eighteenth century. He was also largely responsible for the laying out of the garden, and just as the villa marks a new departure in architectural fashion, so the gardens opened a new chapter in the history of landscape gardening. Gardens of the late seventeenth and early eighteenth century were invariably formal in their arrangements and those belonging to the larger houses were usually built up round long formal avenues and canals, copying in this the style which had been evolved in France by Louis XIV's gardener Le Notre. But the Grand Tour which took many English noblemen to Italy introduced them to the beauty of Classical ruins set in the *campagna*, a beauty which was captured in the paintings of Claude Lorrain and Nicholas Poussin. By comparison, the English formal garden seemed both sterile and unnatural. Kent's painterly eye was sensitive to the qualities of the new style of 'landscape gardening' and at Chiswick he designed for Burlington a garden which mixed a formal framework of avenues and paths with more irregular features. The Chiswick garden was too small for major works of landscaping; rather it was intended to excite the imagination, both by unexpected views and by miniature temples, monuments and other structures.

Villas, being on the whole smaller and cheaper to build than mansion houses, often responded more quickly to changes in taste, and the valley of the

The garden at Chiswick opened a new chapter in the history of landscape gardening in England. William Kent designed for Lord Burlington a garden of moderate size which mixed the traditionally formal framework of avenues and paths with more irregular features. To excite the imagination there were unexpected views, miniature temples and a wilderness.

River Thames which offered easy communication with London and the court saw the building of many villas. Only a year after Chiswick was started, work began on building Marble Hill House at Twickenham, an unusually instructive exemplar of the architectural ideas of the English Palladian school which grew up in the wake of Colen Campbell and Lord Burlington. Marble Hill was intended as the country retreat of Henrietta Howard, Countess of Suffolk and mistress of the Prince of Wales, later King George II. A charming but unhappy woman, the countess enjoyed the friendship of many members of the prince's circle. One of them was Lord Herbert, a man of taste and an amateur of architecture; another was the architect Colen Campbell. Campbell provided the original design, which was adapted by Herbert and built under the supervision of Roger Morris, a protégé of Herbert who became an established architect working mostly in the Palladian style. Marble Hill was closer in spirit to the relatively simple farm-house-villas of Palladio than Burlington's opulent pavilion at Chiswick; the architect's model in so far as he had one was probably Palladio's Villa Emo. The new house was a compact rectangular block of three storeys with a pyramidal roof and a flat representation of a Classical temple front on the entrance façade. The front towards the river had only the simplest of pediments. As at Chiswick, the main rooms were on the first floor and they were proportioned according to geometrical rules. The garden arrangements were quite different. Advice was sought from the poet Alexander Pope, one of the advocates of the new style used at Chiswick, but the principal feature of Lady Howard's garden was a wide open lawn stepping down in grassy terraces towards the river and bounded on either side by regular groves of trees, twice set back so as to reveal as wide a view as possible. To the north, the house was screened from the public road by a plantation of trees whose place has now been taken by playing-fields. There were also several garden buildings punctuating the landscape but these have also disappeared. While it was less elaborate than the garden at Chiswick, the broader arrangement at Marble Hill where the house was consciously laid open to the natural beauty of the Thames is closer in spirit to the later landscape parks of Capability Brown, which have come to be regarded as the natural habitat of Palladian buildings.

During the middle decades of the eighteenth century the Palladian style followed a natural cycle of growth and decay. By the 1760s younger architects

Marble Hill is a small and very perfect villa in the Palladian style, built as a country retreat for Henrietta Howard, Countess of Suffolk, a charming but unhappy woman who was for many years the mistress of King George II. The house was designed by Colen Campbell whose original scheme was altered by Lord Herbert and Roger Morris; it was begun in 1724 and completed in 1729. Although virtually contemporary with Lord Burlington's villa at Chiswick, the garden arrangements were much simpler. Plantations on either side of the garden front are set back by degrees to reveal a prospect of the River Thames.

and more adventurous patrons were looking for other sources of inspiration. Neglecting the Palladian version of Classical architecture, they took an altogether more archaeological approach and inspected the actual ruins of Classical buildings, drawing and measuring as they went. Robert Adam was one architect who followed this course, spending several years in Italy to measure buildings and cultivate potential patrons. Back in England he set out to revolutionise English domestic architecture by replacing the rigidities of the Palladian manner with a new repertoire of architectural ornament drawn from a wide variety of Classical sources. The success of the new style was immediate and within a few years lightness and elegance had become the watchwords of architecture. Adam and his brothers can also take some of the credit, or the responsibility, for introducing stucco as a facing material for buildings. In the late 1760s the old mansion house at Kenwood just north of London was given a new stucco front, whose bareness was relieved by shallow pilasters with Classical ornament typical of the Adam style.

Inspired by the massive Doric temples of Paestum and other towns of Magna Graecia, some bolder spirits pushed beyond the boundaries of Italy to study the ruins of ancient Greece. The Society of Dilettanti was active in promoting these studies and in 1750 its members financed an expedition to Athens by Charles Stuart and Nicholas Revett. The first fruits of this trip appeared in 1762 with the publication of the first volume of *The Antiquities of Athens*. Though immediately recognised as a major work of architectural scholarship, the effect of this and similar works on contemporary architecture was limited. It produced a *gusto Greco* in decoration but the full-blooded Greek revival was a phenomenon of the early nineteenth century.

Shortly after the beginning of the new century, English architecture split itself into two parallel movements – the Greek revival and the Gothic revival. Both were similar in their pursuit of archaeological correctness, which led naturally to the direct copying of historical models, whether Greek temples, Gothic tombs or Tudor country mansions. The beginning of the Greek revival can be dated conveniently to 1804, the year in which Thomas Hope, a rich amateur of architecture, published a diatribe against James Wyatt's scheme for Downing College, Cambridge, pleading for the substitution of a pure Greek Doric design. Hope's extreme Greek attitude was new in England, but he carried

The Grange at Northington in Hampshire is the most immediately striking Neo-Classical house in England, thanks to the great portico overlooking the lake. The portico was added to an older house as part of a programme of improvements carried out between 1804 and 1809 by the architect William Wilkins for the banker Henry Drummond. The brick walls of the seventeenth-century building were completely encased within new cement Classical façades in the newly fashionable Greek taste. Some of the back parts of The Grange have been pulled down in recent years but the small conservatory survives and its elegant Ionic portico makes a pleasing contrast with the austerity of the main building.

the day and Downing was built to the designs of William Wilkins, following the model of the Erectheion in Athens. During the next few years the sculptures taken by Lord Elgin from the Parthenon began to arrive in London and they fuelled a more general enthusiasm for all things Greek. After the end of the Napoleonic War at the Battle of Waterloo in 1815, Greek revival architecture spread rapidly through the whole country. It was particularly popular for churches, public institutions and the smaller kind of private houses.

Immediately following his success at Downing, Wilkins was commissioned by the wealthy banker Henry Drummond to transform his old house called The Grange in Hampshire. The original house was a brick building of the late seventeenth century. Sharing the dislike of red brick which was common at the time, Wilkins clad the whole of the outside with a skin of stone-coloured cement and the broad pilasters and architectural ornament of Greek Doric. He concealed the old basement with a broad stone podium and he added a magnificent Classical portico to the east front facing the lake, copied directly from the so-called Temple of Theseus in Athens. Seen from the lake The Grange looks like a temple, but the illusion was spoilt on the west side by a necessary cluster of servants' quarters and other outbuildings. In 1817 the house was sold to Alexander Baring, another banker, and during the course of the nineteenth century several alterations and additions were made. Most felicitous was the Ladies' Wing ending in a conservatory, designed in 1823 by the young Charles Cockerell, another architect with a bent towards Classical scholarship. The conservatory was later altered but the front with its elegant Greek Ionic portico survived and this little building makes a pleasing contrast with the sterner architecture of the main house. After a period of neglect, The Grange has now been rescued for the nation and the shell of the main building – one of the best Neo-Classical houses in Europe – put into good repair.

Wilkins was a successful architect and The Grange was well known. Sir Charles Monck was a private landowner in Northumberland and the house he designed for himself at Belsay has only recently come to be recognised as a Neo-Classical monument of equal importance. The estate at Belsay had been in the hands of the Middleton family since the 1270s and the fortified house built by them in the late fourteenth century still survives. In 1799 Sir Charles Middleton changed his surname to Monck to fulfil one of the conditions of a bequest which

Sir Charles Monck's country house at Belsay in Northumberland, which he designed for himself in 1806 after a honeymoon spent mostly in Greece. The house was arranged round a central court or atrium like the villas of the ancients and the architecture was an austere personal version of the Greek Doric style. Some distance beyond Sir Charles's house can be seen the ruins of the old family residence, of which the earliest part is a fortified tower house of about 1390.

A long canal marks the main axis of the eighteenth-century part of the gardens at Wrest. At its end is an unusually large and handsome garden pavilion in the Baroque style, designed by Thomas Archer and built 1709–1711.

The present house at Wrest Park in Bedfordshire was designed by the first Earl de Grey in the 1830s to take the place of the old de Grey family mansion. It is wholly French in style, which was something unusual in England at the time, and the gardens next to the house were laid out anew in French-style parterres, though the eighteenth-century formal layout beyond was suffered to remain.

The young Queen Victoria bought the estate at Osborne in 1845 and over the next three years a new house was built in which she, Prince Albert and their children could live a private life. The marvellous view over the Solent reminded Prince Albert of the Bay of Naples, so an Italianate style was chosen for Osborne House, with tall towers and balconies overlooking the sea. The private apartments are contained in a small pavilion (on the right in this view), with a much larger wing for the rest of the royal household and for guests. Both the house and the garden, with its formal terraces and fountains in the Italian Renaissance manner, set new fashions in Victorian Britain.

made him a very wealthy man. His education had given him a taste for drawing and for the Classics, and after his marriage in 1804 he made a honeymoon tour of those parts of Europe not occupied by Napoleon's French armies. One stop was Berlin where the great Classical Brandenburg Gate was just being finished, and the couple also stayed a whole year in Athens. After two years abroad they returned to Northumberland and in 1807 a new house was begun. All the evidence suggests that it was designed by Sir Charles himself. The plan is a perfect square of 100 feet, the architecture simple in the extreme, with plain walls and severe windows. No attempt was made, as at The Grange, to imitate a Greek temple; instead Monck seems to have aimed at a modern version of a Greek or Roman villa. This can best be seen inside, where the rooms are arranged round a two-storey central hall based on a Roman atrium. Belsay was too plain for popular taste. One critic wrote sarcastically, 'I perceive that nakedness and simplicity are now employed as synonymous terms . . . (but) would anyone be so infatuated as to think of improving Venus by removing her eyebrows?' The gardens, partly formed out of the quarry which produced the stone for the house, were more informal and romantic, qualities which were enhanced by the later planting made by Sir Arthur Middleton in Victorian times.

Although the Greek style continued in use for public buildings and institutions till well into the nineteenth century, it was expensive and inflexible. Most country house owners preferred something more obviously romantic. The great majority of big houses in the first half of the century were built in the Tudor style, which gave plenty of scope for picturesque towers and battlements, but could also be made to accommodate large servants' wings, plate glass windows and other modern comforts. An alternative was the Italianate style, derived ultimately from the farmhouses shown in the paintings of Claude Lorrain. In 1845 Queen Victoria and her husband Prince Albert purchased old Osborne House in the Isle of Wight and pulled it down to make way for a large sea-side villa, which would be not a grand palace but a private family retreat from ceremony. Albert greatly admired the art and architecture of Italy and he chose an Italianate style for the new house, with tall towers and verandahs overlooking the sea. He prepared the designs himself, with the help of the master-builder Thomas Cubitt. The private apartments were concentrated in the Pavilion Wing. The much larger building alongside contained the apartments for guests

*W*itley Court in Great Witley was a colossal mansion built for the 1st Earl of Dudley in the 1860s, which incorporated parts of an older house. Gutted by fire in 1937, the building is now a shell, and W.E. Nesfield's elaborate garden survives only in outline.

*The Perseus fountain
on the lawn at
Witley Court is an
exuberant complement to
the early Victorian
grandeur of the main
house.*

and the royal household. It is an arrangement curiously reminiscent of Bolsover Castle, built two hundred years earlier. After the death of Albert in 1861 the widowed queen kept the private apartments at Osborne as he had left them, and as they remain today. The new palace was widely imitated and gave the Italianate style a new lease of life. The gardens were also Italianate and their terraces, stepping down from the house, dotted with fountains and statues in the Renaissance manner, set a new fashion which continued till the end of the century.

One imitator was Witley Court in Worcestershire, which now stands as a ruined but splendid monument to a vanished age of garden parties, shooting expeditions and royal house-guests. At first sight, Witley appears as a huge Victorian palace, but it is the product of repeated rebuildings. The original Jacobean house was never pulled down, but was altered many times, notably in 1683, and again in the early nineteenth century by John Nash, who added a huge portico to the garden front. The final assembly was by Samuel Daukes, who enlarged the house in the 1860s for Lord Ward, who had just been created 1st Earl of Dudley. Daukes added a new wing and made other additions in an early Georgian style, which owned something to the example of an adjoining Georgian church, and something to Michelangelo's *Palazzo dei Conservatori*. Witley is a reminder of the wealth and magnificence of the mid-Victorians, but the house is an empty shell; the interiors were burnt out in 1937. The formal garden laid out by Nesfield survives only as outlines in the grass and the splendid Perseus fountain by James Forsyth is permanently dry.

INDEX

Page numbers in *italic* refer to photographs.

INDEX

Further information on these properties can be obtained from English Heritage, Fortress House, 23 Savile Row, London WIX 2BT

*I*ron Bridge takes its name from this splendid single-arched bridge made of cold-blast iron, which spans the River Severn. The bridge was cast in the works of the famous Coalbrookdale ironmaster, Abraham Darby, who adapted a design by the local architect Thomas Farnolls Pritchard. Finished in 1779, it was the earliest bridge of any size to be made entirely of iron, and stands as a potent symbol of the achievement of early British industry.

BIBLIOGRAPHY

This bibliography is intended as the briefest of guides to further reading. Most of the works named include much more comprehensive lists of relevant writings on their particular subject. In addition, the great majority of English Heritage sites are provided with their own individual guidebooks.

BIBBY, G. *Testimony of the Spade*, Collins, London, 1957. (Although in many respects outdated, this is still the simplest introduction to the early development of archaeology.)

BREEZE, D. J. and DOBSON, B. *Hadrian's Wall*, Penguin, London, 1978.

BUTLER, L. and GIVEN-WILSON, C. *Mediaeval Monasteries of Great Britain*, Michael Joseph, London, 1979.

CLARKE, H. *The Archaeology of Mediaeval England*, Colonnade Books, London, 1984.

DARVILL, T. *Prehistoric Britain*, Batsford, London, 1987.

FRERE, S. *Britannia*, Routledge, London, 1967.

JOHNSON, S. *Late Roman Britain*, Routledge, London, 1980.

PLATT, C. *Castles of Mediaeval England and Wales*, Secker & Warburg, London, 1982.

SUMMERSON, J. *Architecture in Britain 1530–1830*, (6th Edn.) Penguin, London, 1977.